Margaret

Margaret Parry's career has been devoted to the service of literature and cross-cultural understanding, both as a university teacher and as a writer. She is bilingual and publishes in both English and French. She has published widely in the field of her doctoral research on Mauriac and Bergson, on inter-cultural communication, and on a range of contemporary European novelists. She has been a founder member of various associations and journals in which she has played leadership and editorial roles, most notably, the Association Européenne François Mauriac which has been a focus of her activity during the last thirty years. It has members in eighteen countries, and its annual conferences focus on the modern European literary scene.[1] She initiated more recently in this context 'Les Rencontres de la Cerisaie' devoted to contemporary Russian writing. Her current writing is veering more towards religion and literary aesthetics. She is a great lover of French rural life.

---

[1] See: _associationeuropeennefrancoismauriac.blogspot.com/_

For my mother

Margaret Parry

THE WAR POETS AND THE DIARY OF AN ORDINARY TOMMY: CONVERGENCE, CLASS AND TRANSMISSION

AUSTIN MACAULEY PUBLISHERS™

LONDON • CAMBRIDGE • NEW YORK • SHARJAH

A CIP catalogue record for this title is available from the British Library.

ISBN 978-1-78629-263-6 (Paperback)
ISBN 978-1-78629-264-3 (E-Book)
www.austinmacauley.com

First Published (2017)
Austin Macauley Publishers Ltd.
25 Canada Square
Canary Wharf
London
E14 5LQ

Cover illustration based on photograph by the author.
All photographs by the author.

Acknowledgments

My warmest thanks to those who, knowingly or not, have played a part in the emergence of this book:

Jeanne Bernard, Richard Cooper, Véronique de Coppet, Kath Goodman, Keith Hanson, Angela Keeble, Ghislain Lobel, Wendy Mann, Jean Ponthieu, Andrew Spooner, Avril Williams, John Wriggles+.

With thanks too to members of the Austin Macauley editorial and production teams for their friendly help and guidance at each stage of the editing process.

Last and not least, I thank my late mother, Mary Hanson, for ensuring that the little black moleskin notebook one day came into my hands. And above all, I thank my grandfather, Harry Atkinson, for having been the man he was.

Siegfried Sassoon poems courtesy of Barbara Levy Literary Agency.

Contents

Frontispiece

Harry Atkinson (1880-1938)

Les morts veulent vivre ; ils veulent vivre en
vous ; ils veulent que votre vie développe
richement ce qu'ils ont voulu. Ainsi les
tombeaux nous renvoient à la vie.

(Alain, 'Le culte des morts', in *Propos sur
le bonheur*)

The dead want to live; they want to live in you; they want your
life to develop to the utmost
everything they wished for. Thus tombstones
restore us to life.

(Alain, 'The cult of the dead', in *Thoughts on
Happiness*)

We met in the night at half-past one, between
the lines. Liedholz shot at me and I at him, and in the ensuing
tumult he surrendered to me. Before we reached our wire he
told me he
had a wife and three children. In the dug-out we gave him a
whisky. Going to the Brigade with my prisoner at
dawn, the early sun made the land
delightful and larks rose singing from
the plain.
In broken French we discussed Beethoven,
Nietzsche and the International.

(Extract from Herbert Read, *Liedholz*, displayed at Green
Howards Museum exhibition on the Somme, 2016)

Foreword

Over recent years a number of war-time diaries, from the First World War, have been handed in to the Regimental Museum of the Green Howards. They are often brought in by the grandchildren of the authors who rightly think that such documents should be preserved. Most have only a few entries and usually these are concerned with the monotony of long marches, poor billets and even worse food. Some speak of terrible conditions in the front line and occasionally, if a Pal's Battalion, of friends or neighbours they have met.

'The Diary of Harry Atkinson, France 1916' – is of a very different character. He was not a Green Howard but served in the RAMC attached to another Yorkshire Regiment – The King's Own Yorkshire Light Infantry.

So what makes this diary so different?

It is the diary of a mature man. Harry was thirty-four years old when he enlisted. Most of the officers would be at least ten years his junior and no doubt needed to rely upon class consciousness to give them the authority they desired. But that too would change as, in the face of so much terror, they realised that they had more in common with each other than with that which separated them.

Harry's maturity shows itself in so many ways, in the detailed observations which he makes and the wide-ranging interest he shows in what is going on away from the front line. For instance, he is fascinated that the French are still using flails for threshing and that beans are a major crop. His character is clearly formed by his Chapel-going Christian Faith as he can write:

'I was very much struck here by the French people, more like ourselves, very strict at church services each morning at 7.00am. and they paid great attention to the Sabbath Day.'

Remarkably, unlike so many others, his own Faith was not destroyed by his experiences. Perhaps, as he was in the RAMC, he dealt with the consequences of man's inhumanity rather than with inflicting it directly himself. He also did not seek to lose himself in the oblivion of alcohol or the cheap perfume and arms of the local 'Madames'.

His diary was his escape, allowing him to shape the chaos around him into a context where 'normal' life continued, where not all buildings and beauty were destroyed and where people continued to fish and plant and live.

'We visited Beauval. I had a look at the Church. It was a credit to the architects and builders for the beautiful carvings and the stained windows and statues, and the marble arched roof quite out of the ordinary, with a beautiful organ and the player facing the congregation with his back to the organ.'

This is not a man who needed the pen of another to express his thoughts and feelings, not like those of whom Wilfrid Owen wrote when he said, 'I heard the sighs of men that have no skill to speak of their distress.'

Harry Atkinson can both speak of his experiences in the front line of the Battle of the Somme and Arras and also of the things that lay beyond that horizon. He has the language and the imagination to transcend the 'distress' and to celebrate the ordinary continuum of human life. There are the seeds of poetry here.

As well as the actual diary, the book takes the reader a hundred years down the line to the present day and two pilgrimages the author has made to the Somme following in her grandfather's footsteps. Here, Harry's seeds of poetry germinate and come to fruition as the author incorporates her own encounters, emotions and reflections in the particular locations which figure in the diary. The resulting poems, which conclude the book, could be said to be the gift of the grandfather through his granddaughter.

The book combines the personal-poetic and the factual-historic to produce what is, in my mind, an inclusive view which hopefully will contribute in some small way to the emerging 'truth of history' – such a central preoccupation of the war poets.

Canon Richard Cooper,
Chaplain to The Queen
Chaplain to The Green Howards

1

The Way of the Poets

Wilfred Owen's first thoughts, on the outbreak of war, were for the great cultural losses the war would signify for England, the eroding of a civilisation to which the greatest European minds had contributed over the centuries. One is more than a little shocked by the contemptuous attitude he expresses towards the 'English regulars', identified in his mind with the tommies, who lived and had their being outside of this context, at least as he conceived of it:

'I feel my own life all the more precious and more dear in the presence of this deflowering of Europe. While it is true that the guns will effect a little useful weeding, I am furious with chagrin to think that the Minds which were to have excelled the civilization of ten thousand years, are being annihilated – and bodies, the product of aeons of Natural Selection, melted down to pay for political statues. I regret the mortality of the English regulars less than that of the French, Belgian, or even Russian or German armies: because the former are all Tommy Atkins, poor fellows, while the continental armies are inclusive of the finest brains and temperaments of the land.'[2]

My grandfather's Christian name was not Tommy, it was Harry; and his surname was not Atkins, it was Atkinson. This difference, notwithstanding Owen's comment, which he would surely come to regret as a soldier and officer fighting alongside the very tommies he had slighted, pinpointed for me, on a personal plane, the issue of class and human difference which the war would highlight, but to set in motion at the same time changes deriving from a changed consciousness on the part of so many individuals, which in the course of a generation would affect the evolution and structure of English society.

Harry Atkinson, whose war diary is the subject of this narrative, seems to me to have been one of these individuals. His mind, through the very act of writing, took a leap forward, discovered, set in motion new impulses and aspirations which, if not immediately apparent to him, would seek through time to come into their own. He surely returned home from the war a different man, more culturally aware and with a deepened perception of life, ready to affect the more sensitive amongst his family and entourage. Of his three daughters whose lives in those far-distant years were still dominated by the mill and the mine and by the ever-present threat of illness and poverty, my mother, privileged more than her elder sisters by her education,

---

[2] From Wilfred Owen, S*elected Letters*, quoted by Nicholas Murray in *The Red Sweet Wine of Youth: The Brave and Brief Lives of the War Poets*, Little, Brown, 2010, pp.140-141.

had an especial relationship with him. Moving on a generation, one of my deepest memories or 'impressions' of childhood is of the rows of poetry books lining the top two shelves of our living-room bookcase. Thus it is that new genes, new passions, are born. I like to think that in our case the war played no small part in the process.

The notebook in which Harry Atkinson kept his day-to-day jottings is a diary, no more than that. Whatever my desire as his granddaughter writing a hundred years after the events described not to romanticize (a temptation all the greater since he died several years prior to my birth), it pleased me even so, as I looked closer into the facts, to discover that he had lived and 'fought' in such close proximity to several of the war poets. On that memorable morning of the first of July, the official start of the battle of the Somme, and close to the village of Serre where he came face to face with the true 'horrors of war' for the first time, he was carrying the wounded from Basin Wood to Observation Wood only a few hundred yards from where, in a field across the road, Wilfred Owen would at a later point lie down in the grass and write a letter to his mother. John William Streets, by birth, situation, temperament and religion so similar to my grandfather, had fallen in this sector on this same ill-fated morning, and was buried at Colincamp, a stone's throw from Bus where Harry Atkinson was billeted; (it is probable that Streets was billeted in the same village). Edmund Blunden arrived at Couin – an important landmark in the diary for the change of moral tone and atmosphere it reflects – a couple of days after my grandfather had left, to traverse during the battalion's ongoing marches the Bassée Canal sector, close to the place where Blunden had engaged in such bitter fighting and which he had described as a 'slaughter yard'[3]. In early April of the year following, Siegfried Sassoon was on the road to Arras, not very far from where my grandfather's battalion had approached for the Arras offensive[4]. And Harry Atkinson arrived at Arras, whose devastation he describes so graphically, only a short time after the tragic, untimely death of Edward Thomas. There are undoubtedly other poets I could mention with whom he might have been in close proximity.

The Somme, then, was a great mixing-ground. Yet Harry Atkinson would have had no consciousness that he was rubbing shoulders with such poets. It would have made no difference if he had. He was a miner, whose conscience had led him to volunteer for Kitchener's army to serve king and country. He had a job of work to do; he would do it and hopefully return home where life would resume much the same as before. Just as John William Streets expected to do. Two Northeners, though in different regiments or units, who for one brief moment on 1 July had been so close physically on the battlefield.

Of the various like-minded 'others' that through a chance encounter my grandfather might have come into contact with – one imagines a fellow soldier passing by one evening at Bus when he is lost in his jottings and striking up a conversation with him – it is JW Streets I

---

[3] Edmund Blunden, *Undertones of War*, Penguin, 1928, p.28.
[4] Sassoon was repatriated on 16 April after being wounded by a sniper.

would most like him to have met. Streets was a miner like himself, one of twelve children (Harry Atkinson was one of eleven), a devout Methodist, who had renounced his aspirations as a poet in order to work and support his siblings. Streets was killed on the first morning of the Somme. He had survived the first wave of the assault but returned to the battlefield to aid a wounded comrade; his body was found in no-man's-land. When, at a particularly moving point in his diary, in the midst of the account of his front-line activities aiding and transporting the wounded, Harry Atkinson evokes the courage, nobility and self-sacrifice of those who put their comrades before themselves, describing one severely wounded soldier whose life was rapidly draining out of him yet who doggedly carried the body of a fellow soldier along the trench for more than fifty yards, it is of JW Streets that I think.

Harry Atkinson was in the Royal Army Medical Corps (RAMC), a member of the 94th field ambulance attached to the 31st Division which included the Leeds, Bradford, and Accrington pals (Streets was one of the Sheffield pals); he worked in close proximity to the 15th battalion (the 1st Leeds pals) of the West Yorkshire Regiment. In the winter of 1915 he trained at Aldershot, Rolestone (near Salisbury), Exeter, and Plymouth, before sailing to Egypt (Port Said) with the other pals' groups referred to, for what appears to have been a relatively easy and relaxed period of duty protecting the Suez Canal. They left Port Said on 1 March, 1916 for Marseilles and the onward journey to the Somme.

Why did Harry Atkinson join the RAMC? Was the decision made for him due to his age (born in 1880, he was thirty-four on the outbreak of war and thus older than the average recruit), and also perhaps due to his experience in health and safety work in the mine? Or was it at his own request as a deeply religious man, who conscientiously objected to the exigency to kill and to look upon others as his enemy? Occasional comments in the diary would suggest the latter as the more likely explanation. It seems relevant to consider too whether being in the RAMC facilitated his keeping of a diary or log, or whether he would have kept one regardless of his posting. Whilst the view expressed to me by one military man that the RAMC lads had an 'easier time of it' is open to question, it is perhaps true to say that the more diverse and sometimes individual activities and responsibilities attached to working in a field ambulance gave him the opportunity to keep a diary more regularly than he might have done as a 'tommy in the field'. That there was some call to write, however, which he would have found the means to satisfy one way or another, seems hardly to be in doubt. The shock and excitement of change, of exposure to the new, especially to a different culture, but also to a disrupted and disorientating universe which, for the man of faith that he was, dictated the need for being with, or retreat into, the self as a sort of safe haven – the only known element in a sea of unknowing – all of these factors were a catalyst.

Would the majority of war poets I have mentioned including others of their category ever have admitted or even considered, coming as they did from a different class, that these ordinary tommies (or individuals amongst them), to whom as officers they issued their daily commands, could have wielded a pen as they did, that they could have felt instincts, impulses welling up in them which sought expression in the written word? To say what? Even in the case of the recognized poets the motivation remains obscure or takes some considerable time to recognize itself, unless aided and abetted by 'blighty'. Sassoon and Owen, benefitting from their daily contact at Craiglockhart where they had been repatriated due to shell-shock, shocked indeed by their exposure to the cruel and wasteful loss of so many young lives, were not slow to realize the urge through poetry to combat the complacency of those back home, especially those in positions of power and authority, who had no conception of the mass slaughter and wholesale destruction being carried out. To tell 'the truth about war' became their clarion call, and with this came the stimulation of searching for, of chiselling from the bedrock new words, new forms of language to state the 'truth' in all its brute reality.

But there was a contrasting urge too, perhaps more spontaneous, less consciously articulated, one recognizable in a significant number of the war poets. It can be summed up in the word 'nostalgia'. Many of the poems, stimulated for example by the sound of a bird song in a lull between the roaring of guns, or the glimpse of a clump of wild flowers peeping up through the rubble, were a lament, an elegiac refrain for the homeland – for its country lanes and villages and inns, for its meadows and woods and native fauna and flora, all of which they might never see again.

There was also that more general trait, common to any true writer and poet, to sympathize with humanity's lot. As officers and men were drawn closer together by the experience of the trenches and class differences were

25

effaced, poets like Blunden and Owen (both of whom wrote in prose too), warming to the courage, stamina and good humour of the ordinary soldier were only too ready to testify to such qualities and speak for those who could not speak for themselves, at least in a language which would publicize if not immortalize their greatness and nobility. One can ask oneself in passing whether Wilfred Owen would have written a poem like 'Miners'[5] if he had not had this experience of class interdependency and solidarity and learned to empathize with his men in this way.

Harry Atkinson, not a poet but already with the stirrings of the poet in him, was no different from his illustrious comrades as regards a certain humanist vision which speaks through his narrative – his sustaining belief in the power of the human spirit and intelligence to fight on and endure. What marks him as different, though, is the absence of any suggestion of nostalgia for the homeland. This is to be explained in part, no doubt, by the official constraints imposed with regard to what could and could not be written down in a personal act of communication; and if one military historian I spoke to is right, personal diaries were strictly forbidden. So there is no mention of home and family, except for an odd reference to his 'pal' brother or other 'lads' or 'boys' from his home town encountered in combat or billet zones. Harry Atkinson's mind was almost of necessity focussed on the present and for much of the diary there seems to have been no real instinct to escape from it as he wrote. Harry Atkinson was a man with his feet set firmly on the ground. He was alert to all that was going

---

[5] See Epilogue.

on around him, intelligent and questioning, however minimal his education, though one should not underestimate the role of church and chapel here.

Why and for whom he wrote the diary must remain a matter of conjecture. Undoubtedly there was his sense of the importance of the historic moment and his desire to record it, not to let it pass into oblivion, as too a sense of the apocalyptic, biblical nature of the event. One wonders too, whatever the official taboo, whether there was not encouragement from certain more enlightened quarters to keep a diary as a means of coming to terms with the experience[6].

Whatever the impulsion, much of the diary seems to transcend any factual, historic purpose. It is personal and, interestingly, the most personal part concerns his discovery of France and the excitement of being in a foreign country and culture. Unlike the war poets, Harry Atkinson comes across not as a man of nostalgia, brought by the experience of exile, and of the worst imaginable kind, to a deeper love and appreciation of his native land. He was, as the French would say, 'un homme d'ouverture'. His imagination was opened and his horizons enlarged by the adventure of cultural difference. He was stimulated by ways different from English ways, by sights which went beyond his normal experience and uplifted his spirit. For any intelligent, open-minded working-class man this was surely natural. Unlike the poets, most of them from the upper classes,

---

[6] I am reminded here, in the modern era, of the use to which diaries are put by language students on their year abroad, serving as a means of acculturation and reducing culture shock.

27

Harry Atkinson had not travelled before. Except for cricket matches – he was an ardent and talented cricketer, though I have not been able to verify the family legend that he once played for Yorkshire – he would hardly have ventured beyond the small West Riding town where he lived and worked. This was his first foray into a foreign country and, the experience of the battlefield and tending to the wounded apart, he was stimulated by what he saw. Undoubtedly, this was the source of new linguistic urges in him and gave a poetic dimension to certain of his entries.

This, then, is a celebration of my grandfather's World War 1 diary. But it is more than that. It is also about the divide of class and how the war broke down divisions, social and educational, paving the way for a new cultural epoch: this, not only through bringing the upper classes into contact with the grit and heroism, the dignity and humanity of the ordinary man, which most had probably never cared to think about before; but also because the war, through exposing the ordinary soldier to horrors unimaginable, to sufferings both mental and physical, but also to new landscapes of the imagination, liberated the desire in them – and how many other diaries equally precious yet unknown are there to uplift and inspire us two generations down the line? – to say things they had never said before and, through the adventure of words, to respond to sounds more resonant than those they had yet heard, to rhythms they did not know to be rhythms?

… Just as Wilfred Owen's poetic imagination was liberated by his exposure to men different from himself, from another class, whom he had never truly seen or known before. It needed close cohabitation with the ordinary soldiers in the trenches for him to learn to empathize with them and find them true subjects for poetry, stripped to the essentials of their humanity. So he came to write poems which, when one refers back to the opening citation of this chapter, one would never have thought him capable of writing[7]. Many of these are born of the comradeship and fraternity experienced in the front-line trenches. But it is his poem 'Miners', more allusive, more mythical and timeless in the images it conveys of 'whisperings' and 'murmurings' and 'writhing for air' of men below ground, which brings home to me the wonder and significance of Harry Atkinson's little black moleskin. That, not only for what the notebook reveals of a mind freed from the normal routines of living, exercised by emotions and experiences entirely new which sought to translate themselves into words; but also for the content of the 'translation' itself, which adds to our sum of knowledge of the war experience as contributed by a direct participant in the events described.

One can not underestimate the documentary value of Harry Atkinson's diary which, together with other personal testimonies of a similar nature still no doubt in many cases waiting to be uncovered, adds to a certain 'truth about war' more authentic and compelling than the objective, scientific accounts of history books. A survey of the main themes and structure of the narrative, as reflecting the dynamic of a mind and sensibility interacting with history and attaining to a new freedom

[7] See Epilogue.

of expression, will serve, in the next chapter, as a preliminary to the diary itself.

2

From the Somme to Arras: The Testimony of a Participant Observer

The diary, a small black moleskin notebook measuring three and a half inches by six with small squared paper, most likely French in origin, covers seventy-six pencil-written pages in mostly neat handwriting, odd lapses suggesting tiredness or haste. The title page bears the author's name and address in the top right-hand corner, very neatly written, and the centre of the page in uncharacteristic scrawl the one word 'France' accompanied by the barely decipherable date 1916. The entries start on 1 March, 1916 with the troops 'steaming away' from Port Said, and end on 21 June, 1917, after two months' service at the Battle of Arras. The larger part of the diary, following a detailed account of the sea journey to Marseilles and the onward journey to Picardy, and with interludes of marching and rest periods, focuses on the Battle of the Somme – some fifty pages. Thirty-four place names are mentioned, occasional ones – key transit points for the troops – more than once. One can thus follow the writer's itinerary closely.

The density of material detail – in addition to dates and distances and occasionally time by the clock, information about the weather (they arrived in Picardy to extreme cold and snow, followed by persistent rain so that on his first foray into the trenches he found himself 'knee deep in water'), about billets which more than once he humorously refers to as 'open-air treatment', about the discomforts of marching (twenty-two miles with a ten-pound pack on one's back was no fun), the frustrations too when they were not told where they were going and for what and which he laughs off with a comment on the 'tourist division', the recording of all the sights and the sounds, particularly on or close to the battlefield... all of this, accompanied by personal reflections, gives a graphic sense of presence, of being there at the event. This is especially the case on the first four days of the Somme when a certain air of wonder and unknowing, reminiscent at moments of great fictional accounts of battle (as he splashes through the trenches, almost with the amazed bewilderment of a child in some adventure labyrinth, I was reminded of Fabrice Del Dongo at Waterloo[8]), adds to the sense of immediacy. As do his powers of description which, in places, contain strong echoes of the Bible.

Harry Atkinson and the accompanying battalion(s) arrived at Bus, a 'dirty and dilapidated' village only a short distance from the front line and 'within range of the German guns' on 4 April. Two days later he had his first experience of a bombardment, two hours during which 'the earth shook and the elements were ablaze'.

---

[8] In the novel of the 19th century French writer, Stendhal, *The Charterhouse of Parma* (*La Chartreuse de Parme*).

For the next few weeks he was busy with the ambulance unit developing hospital accommodation to receive the increasing numbers of wounded, an activity not without its moments of danger as when he had to go to the 'danger zone' to retrieve construction materials from buildings destroyed by German shells. Then came news of preparations for an 'important movement', and on the night of 30 June he was moved up to a front-line dressing station, in effect no more than a rat infested barn which during the night came under such heavy shell fire that they had to move to a cellar where he spent a sleepless night waiting for morning and the 'start for Berlin'. That 'memorable morning' (as he calls it) of 1 July when at 7.30 the whistle blew for the lads to 'go over the lid', not before he had observed with his own eyes their own bombardment which had grown more terrific, bursting over the German lines which now were 'one mass of smoke'. If, to begin with, he is in the relative cover of the dressing station watching for 'the patients [who] were beginning to stream down the road', it is not long before he is in the thick of the action himself, 'shot and shell flying in all directions' and causing him to 'duck and dive all the time'. A stretcher-bearer now, assigned to carry patients from Basin Wood to Observation Wood, the catastrophe – whatever the rumours soon circulating of the successful advance of the 'boys' over the German lines – is only too apparent. Called to the assistance of the regimental stretcher-bearers, the few remaining ones, that is, for 'most of them had fallen doing their gallant duty', he now finds himself in 'the first line of the trenches blown level in places', 'walking over dead bodies and trees and machine guns and all kinds of obstructions and bombs by the dozens'. In view of the Germans, the work is 'difficult and dangerous', 'most cruel and arduous'.

These first four or five days of the Somme offensive must have passed very quickly for him. One dramatic moment follows another, as when with five of his 'chums' he is called by an officer to go to the rescue of three koylies[9], on the bare edge of survival after being stuck in a shell-hole for three days. Out in no-man's-land, exposed once again to the 'lights and rat tat of [enemy] guns', it is like a game of 'hide and seek', calculating the moment to 'dive' and 'escape' into a shell-hole 'before the lights burst into their brilliance'. But the climax of the episode, reserved for the end, is not the rescue itself, however rewarding, even thrilling this must have been; it is when, on his first dive into a shell-hole to avoid death, he has the surprise of finding himself with a comrade, 'in a kneeling position... either praying or looking over the top'. He speaks to him, shakes him, and realizes he is dead.

The extremes of emotion in this game of hide and seek between life and death are ever present. Harry Atkinson is too restrained a man to describe them directly. But they are communicated to the reader through what we may term a mode of poetic suggestion deriving unconsciously from the graphic power of words and their combinations.

The diary continues in similar, if less dramatic vein, for Harry Atkinson, despite two returns to the battle zone after intervening periods of 'rest' (yet as he characteristically says at one point, 'you can always find work cleaning up these rest camps'), was not called

---

[9] Kings Own Yorkshire Light Infantry.

again to work at the front-line trenches – probably the luck of the draw. Except for a lucky escape at Arras, but as a 'civilian' now who has come to the town centre to see the desolation with his own eyes, there are not the moments of intensity as during his front-line experience from the first to the fifth of July. Inevitably too, as the months pass and the war drags on and the wounded and sick arrive at the hospital in ever-increasing numbers – it is in the hospital that most of his next main phase of duty is spent – morale deteriorates. It is to be noted in fact that on 26 January – the date significant enough for him to record the event – he put in for a transfer to the Royal Engineers Railways.

Yet the writing remains as engaging as ever for the different experiences it recounts, both personal and general, and for the insights it provides into the ups-and-downs of the war. Following those terrible first days at the Somme, the unit is withdrawn from the fighting zone and after several stops and starts arrives for a two-month rest period at a rural retreat called Calonne-sur-la-Lys further to the north. They returned to the front in mid-November to a place called Couin, only a couple of kilometres or so from their first billets at Bus, where they 'were once more amongst the noise and roar of guns'. They spent two months here and his work in the ambulance unit was very different. Unlike seventy-five of his comrades (roughly a third of the unit) called back to assist on the front line and by the side of whom he considered himself 'fortunate', Harry Atkinson was engaged principally in hospital work.

Even if he considered himself 'fortunate', a certain dejection is soon apparent. He was working here with the sick – to begin with about four hundred of them –

rather than the wounded. Amongst these were German prisoners-of-war working on a nearby quarry who, he states – the first sign of his diminishing morale – 'seemed as fed up with the job as we were'. This was in spite of the fact that for once he had some home comforts – a spring mattress and plenty of blankets, which gave him a decent 'kip' (to use the latest jargon). For the first time too there are signs of a latent class consciousness, undoubtedly corrosive. He does not conceal a certain bad feeling with regard to the officers who, most of the time, had 'as much to eat and drink as they wanted and every other comfort'. He is critical in particular of the commanding officer who, no doubt to please his superiors, would resist no efforts to increase the workload of the hospital workers, already under-strength by seventy men. (Fifty of the men were diverted to another ambulance to assist with road construction and quarrying stone.) So, instead of the boredom he might normally have felt when he was given mundane practical tasks to do (here lighting and odd jobs) – for he was essentially a 'people's person' motivated by a sense of duty to others – here it was rather a sense of relief; for those working in the wards, having seventy to a hundred patients to look after day and night between two or three of them, 'the patients could not get the care and comfort which was needed'. He finds himself involved even so, giving his own observations and views on the scabies epidemic now ravaging the troops and accounting for most of the five hundred to six hundred regular admittances.

Harry Atkinson was decidedly not happy at Couin and he was relieved like everyone else – due to overwork and poor management there was unrest generally – when they were moving on. After a circular six weeks' forced march in the winter cold of January and February 1917, which included his second 'main' rest period in terms of the personal benefits and pleasure he derived from it, at the town of Beauval near Doullens – his precise dating indicates other prolonged stays in one place or another yet which brought no comment from him – they found themselves back in 'the same old place Couin, the same hospital CRS'. The fear of renewed fighting in the sector proving false, they were soon on the move again, this time further north, and spent two months (15 March to 10 May) marching from one place to another 'not knowing [their] destination', in reserve for a time at Vimy Ridge and eventually arriving in the vicinity of Arras. They took over trenches on 10 May for what would turn out to be the last days of the Battle of Arras; it ended on 16-17 May.

Arras was a different experience yet again, at least as recorded in his diary. Once again it was his lot or good fortune not to be assigned to the front line for the recovery and transporting of the wounded: there were a number of casualties in his unit, including their first deaths; the victims he records by name. With thirty others in his unit, Harry Atkinson remained back at headquarters, where he must have had a certain freedom of movement. Now it is the urban devastation which claims his attention and provides the element of drama in the narrative. He soon realized they were 'in the roughest place' they had visited on all their 'travels' (a word to be noted), 'as every house was a mass of ruins for miles'. With the same intelligent curiosity as he reveals in his rest periods, and which had recently sent him to explore a pit head on their first arrival in the coal mining districts of the north, he was soon paying a visit to Arras itself 'to see the destruction which had been wrought there on 3 May'. Ironically – and there is a certain humour in the telling – once again at the front yet out of the danger zone, he comes as close to death as he has ever been. After only a few minutes' leisurely strolling he detects 'music in the air' and finds himself running for his life as German shells rain down, with 'bits of shrapnel [coming] close by and stones flying in the air'.

This is the climactic point of Harry Atkinson's narrative. The diary winds down after this point, to end a few lines later, not without indicating, however, in a rapid summing-up of the unit's movements during the weeks following, when their thoughts focus more and more on leave, that whatever the official dating – 16 May – of the end of the Battle of Arras, the fighting was far from over; his division and the two ambulances attached to it were still in the line a month later[10].

The experience at Arras is climactic in another sense and suggests how anxiously, if partly for hidden reasons, he must have awaited leave: it is in revealing the emergence of the hardened soldier in him who can take pleasure now in seeing a German plane brought to earth. The contrast is striking with the morning of his first arrival in France at Marseilles fifteen months earlier, when he had been so reassured by the contented looks on the faces of the German prisoners-of-war, his first sight of the enemy or – as he preferred to use the word – 'foe'.

---

[10] The memory of one family member suggests he was repatriated on health grounds sometime between 1917 and 1918, but official records indicate he was still on active service in 1918.

Yes, as he had noted on his first visit to a cemetery near Bus, 'the tender hearts seem to get hardened by such sights'. Harry Atkinson, a man of deep religious faith, undoubtedly struggled throughout these long months of war service to remain the man he was, or thought himself to be when he had joined up. As will now be seen, the diary sheds interesting light on the role played by the 'rest periods' – perhaps too by the act of reflection and expression and by the services of army chaplains – in helping him to retain a sense of moral equilibrium.

As indicated, two rest periods figure predominantly in the diary: Calonne-sur-la-Lys, which followed his period of duty at Bus and the first days of the Somme, and Beauval, which came between his two periods of hospital duty at Couin. They reveal Harry Atkinson, however naturally sociable he might be, as a rather solitary figure who enjoys peace and tranquillity above all else and employs his new-found leisure in ways different from most of his fellows.

Calonne-sur-la-Lys, a rural, well-irrigated backwater a few miles north of Béthune, surrounded by flat marshlands and agricultural land, was above all for him a haven of quiet after the incessant cacophony of the guns. There is no more telling and poetic statement on the profound, transformative effect on his morale (as on that of his fellows) than this one: 'Here we were like giants refreshed with new wine; it was like heaven to get back once more to civilisation.' Apart from organized activities (sports, concerts) and fishing – though with characteristic humour he describes the fish as being as slippery and elusive as the Germans – he spent his time alone. He does not, at the first opportunity, dash off with the lads to the nearby town of Merville, an attractive town offering every manner of distraction. He spends his time roaming the country lanes, watching the peasant women at work in the fields. Unlike so many of the war poets, whose renewed contact with nature aroused a sense of nostalgia for England, the home-land – or for an idealized image of it – Harry Atkinson experienced rather a sense of belonging, of being at home in proximity to these 'French people more like ourselves'. Whatever the differences of habits and customs which he took pleasure recording, he soon felt himself in the presence of people with whom he could identify. Perhaps a certain element of nostalgia does come into it as he describes ways long lost to the English – harvesting techniques and the use of the flail, for example, or, reminiscent now of his own experience, the killing of the pig, upon which he lavishes such detail. But it is the stimulation of difference, now that he finds himself for the first time in a foreign land, which feeds his imagination and observations, and the fact that, despite the differences, he can feel such a sense of relaxation and intimacy before those he is observing, attributable in part to their capacity for unremitting toil and disciplined endeavour, also for their strict religious observances. The diary serves at this point as an interesting social rather than military document. Yet to limit it to such terms is to underestimate its value. For the diary here is not so much an accumulation of facts as of personal impressions. It is these which make up the charm of the narrative, or rather picture. One has here the passing impression, through the author's strong identification with his subject – particularly the women bent seemingly motionless in toil – of being implanted into a painting by Jean-François Millet, *The Gleaners* or *The Angelus*.

At Beauval, an attractive semi-rural, semi-industrial town on the main Doullens-Amiens road, with high hills rising above it on one side and rolling green countryside on the other, Harry Atkinson's mind and imagination were opened and enriched in a different way. Beauval had served as a transit point for his unit at least four times on their travels to, from, and around the front; but this was the first occasion he had stayed there for any length of time. The main feature in the town to have caught his attention and which he hastened now to look at more closely was the church, which he does not know whether to refer to as a 'church' or a 'cathedral', a hesitation understandable for one who has not travelled before and certainly not to a cathedral city, who has never in fact seen beyond his own low-built, modest local church; (the church at Beauval is indeed a huge and grandly decorated one for a small town). He was clearly overwhelmed by the experience – by its dimensions and the magnificence of its interior. His spontaneous enjoyment and aesthetic appreciation are evident in his comments on the quality of the architecture, on the beautiful carvings and stained-glass windows and statues, and on the unusual marble arched roof and organ, whose player, strangely, sat facing the congregation with his back to his instrument or the main part of it (a detail which would suggest he had attended a church service there). The inspiration he found in the church undoubtedly affected his view of the town generally which, despite being 'degraded' by long occupation by troops – this went for 'the people' too – he found 'rather beautiful and clean'. His state of mind is such that, despite his view (whatever the 'cheery news' from the *Daily Mail* might suggest to the contrary) that 'the end of the war seemed as far off as ever', he can feel that he is 'making the best of it' and 'look ahead to brighter and better times'. Beauval, with its artistic treasures and, on the part of the beholder, the 'liberty' to enjoy them, provides a moment of light, of moral illumination to counter the diminishing morale of the diary's later pages. This, despite the 'rough weather' of January 1917 with its almost incessant snow and the fact that once again for billets they had to contend with 'the fresh air treatment'. But for Harry Atkinson, it would seem, such inconveniences are as nothing once beauty is present. Was this his first encounter with culture (more broadly conceived than religion) as an antidote to human suffering?

Moments of poetry, then, are discernible at almost every stage of the diary. Yet clearly this is only one dimension of the narrative, if, arguably, the most important, for beyond the factual detail it betrays the voice of the author himself and confers a certain unity to the whole. The diary will remain even so, for all perhaps but his most intimate readers, a war document first and foremost, providing a wealth of observations on significant aspects of the war experience. To the military historian it adds an essential personal dimension to the objective information contained in the official RAMC and regimental diaries, with its detailed, often day by day and precisely dated commentary on the movements and itinerary of the RAMC unit attached to the 31st Division: the first-hand experience it communicates of working in the front lines, its specifying of locations and numbers of wounded and sick arriving at particular dressing and clearing stations and hospitals, the information it provides on billets and rest places and the way the tommies spent their leisure time, on the changing morale of the troops and on social and class attitudes, on novel (for soldiers on the ground) experiences such as seeing an information balloon or engagements in the air and witnessing a plane coming corkscrewing to earth[11]. The diary casts an interesting light too on the concept of 'pals', the author meeting up at the most unlikely moments with friends and a brother from home, home, interestingly, not so much Birstall, the town itself from where he came[12] (a small enough place in itself) as a particular and limited location within the town: Mount Top, with its own very distinct identity and about which a whole book could be written[13].

Of especial importance too, on a military plane, are the insights the diary provides on the work of an ordinary soldier or tommy in the RAMC. As one watches the navvying interludes of recuperating bricks

---

[11] Note Charles H.Horton's comment in his memoir, *Stretcher Bearer*, Lion Books, 2013 – he was also in the RAMC – 'The Medical Corps can surely claim to be the most widely ignored of all branches of the services', p.21; see also p.22 for his evaluation of RAMC work as compared with that of combatants in the field.

[12] He was actually born in West Rounton, well outside the industrial West Riding, in an agricultural area close to the Cleveland hills and North York moors. Views like Roseberry Topping may have shaped his imagination as a child.

[13] See Malcolm Clegg, 'They're the top', chapter 9 in *Echoes from Birstall past*, Malcolm Clegg with Smith Settle, Yeadon, 2006.

and stones from bombed sites, of constructing 'huts' and dressing stations and hospitals or adapting existing buildings for the same, of managing lighting or oil and paint supplies for the hospital wards, it is easy to underestimate the extreme emotional stress to which they were so frequently subjected – surely as much as the average soldier on the field – as, unarmed, they recuperated the wounded on the field, or busied around the clearing and dressing stations and the wards, full to overflowing with the mutilated and suffering and often dying. Perhaps the periods of navvying were so timed – assuming enlightenment on the part of commanding officers – to provide alleviation from such trauma which, as Harry Atkinson's diary indicates, could 'harden' the most 'tender hearts'.

We are brought back to the question of Harry Atkinson the man, and it is the expression of the man, gradually emerging as a living, rounded character who engages our interest and emotions as a living, moving witness to events. The overriding aspect of his person, evident from the very first lines but at almost every stage of the narrative too, is his faith, which clearly carried him through. It is almost the voice of an Old Testament prophet – the only literary language to which he would have been regularly exposed – intimidating in its force and strength, which introduces the narrative, distancing him somewhat from the reader: 'I proposed in my heart to trust in the Lord and not be afraid of the terrors by night nor the pestilence by day'. The tone continues, but at the level now of his personal conscience as he grapples with the problem of alcohol, having signed the temperance pledge. Chilled no doubt to the marrow as they settle into the cold, unheated and unlighted carriages which transport him from Marseilles, he turns down two cups of tea because of the warming rum added to it; only six lines later, however, he has clearly broken the pledge, admitting that 'a drink of warm tea was a treasure to us'. Sunday too was a problem for him and there is a certain self-protective irony in his comment on 'what great things are done in the army on Sunday'. Yet Sunday too, depending on the situation, might bring respite and solace in the form of a service conducted by an army chaplain. When he talks of the 'good times spiritually' they had on such occasions, one can only feel how short-sighted was the attitude of an officer like Robert Graves who expressed such reservations concerning the role of the chaplains[14].

This high moral attitude on Harry Atkinson's part might suggest a severe, narrow-minded, even sanctimonious character who stood apart from his fellows. On the contrary, he emerges as a good-natured, tolerant and non-judgmental man – even on the question of French drink which he fears will be the 'ruination' of so many of the 'lads' – who enjoys sports and concerts as much as any man, but whose humanity raised him perhaps somewhat above the average in an instinctive concern to preserve the best human values. He is saddened, for example, during his experience at the front as he sees now an officer, now a tommy showing exemplary bravery, by the thought that they will be deprived of any chance of a military cross because there is no person of authority there to give an account of

---

[14] See Robert Graves, *Goodbye to all that*, Penguin Books, 1960, pp.157-159.

them. Good deeds, as expressive of the best in human nature, are to be rewarded. Not that he is a man for public show or honours. Human kindness, compassion, self-denial which remain hidden from the public gaze are what move him most. Despite the horrors and inhumanities of war which the diary records, it is a testimony most essentially to the nobility of the ordinary soldier who shows a sudden capacity to rise above his condition. In this lies the poetic dimension of the narrative – those glimmers of light flashing through the darkness which move Harry Atkinson to use words, language he would not normally have used and in what was probably the only sustained piece of writing he ever wrote. The miracle is that it survived, for the enlightenment of future generations and, for the present writer, the only contact with the grandfather I had not known.

3

France 1916: The War Diary of Harry Atkinson (1880-1938)

My visit from Egypt to France (March 1st 1916)

We steamed away from Port Said. I had the pleasure of meeting one or two of my friends, Lft J S Auty & Hy Lonsdale, and the despondence that was born upon me on boarding the ship vanished as we sped along. We had a pleasant time in the day time but when night came on we had to go below. It was no pleasant feeling, especially for those who had not committed their cares to their Heavenly Father for their safe keeping. I had purposed in my heart to trust in the Lord and not be afraid of the terrors by night nor the pestilence by day. Quite different from the Nestor, the Minneapolis [had] no electric lights by night, not even a match. We had to get into our dungeons the best way we could, fix up our hammocks before dark and feel our way the best we could. I well remember trying, or having to go on deck one night and a terrible struggle it was, as many of the boys slept on the floor and the only way to get out safely was to go on your hands and knees and back the same way, with a little more difficulty in finding your hammock. But by counting tables etc. we had to manage, and sometimes we had a disturbance by someone letting your hammock down just for fun, but it was rather dangerous.

Food was poor and scarce but the one thing we could praise our ship for was her speed. We had about 200 horses on board and most of the staff officers. The ship above deck was well equipped for officers' hospital etc. and it was my misfortune to visit the hospital each day, which was carried on by our ambulance, to have my leg dressed, which was a result of the sports in Egypt or I might say the pillow fight. But by the rest of the voyage I was able to get about right again. There was not very much excitement during our few days' sail but we were in very dangerous waters. We got news one day that we were passing over the place where a ship had been sunk the day previous and the crew told us they had been chased the last few journeys they had made. [It] would [be] a very good catch for the enemies to sink useful vessels like her and many of the crew were of the impression they were going to London after they had dispersed with us and were not to come aboard her again. But we found out later they were disappointed and had to make another journey for troops. Which was unfortunately her last, as she was sunk on leaving port again after delivering her charge and a lot of the crew were drowned.

We reached Malta on March 4th at 2.00p.m. and anchored outside awaiting orders. We were surrounded by ships and the usual signalling performance was gone through by our captain but we did not go into harbour as we only stayed until 3.00p.m. then once more began our

We reached Malta on March 4th at 2.00p.m.

journey. On Sunday we had a Wesleyan service by our chaplain Mr Martin and also a medical inspection, which was getting a regular occurrence for us and we were getting quite used to them. And once more we saw land and we kept in sight of land for the rest of the journey.

On Monday the 6th of March at 1.00p.m. we arrived at Marseilles. We had a destroyer came out to meet us at a tremendous speed, and the entering of the harbour was a beautiful scene, amongst which was our first appearance of our enemies of which there were a large number of German prisoners employed in this harbour. They were kept fully employed and seemed quite happy and contented with their work. We were told there were 5000 of them and at night they were lodged in a large ship. There were many captured ships in dock. We had to spend the night on our ship but the artillery began to remove their guns which had been in position throughout the voyage for a safeguard against our foes.

But in the early morning of the 7th we were up and doing, busy unloading all our equipment and luggage etc., and we had quite a busy forenoon transferring from ship to train. We left Marseilles at 2.30p.m. for a trip – as we had been told a two days' journey by train – if I may use that expression. With stops and starts we did get to our journey's end. But with all the lovely scenery it was a miserable journey. We were in carriages but with very little chance of sleep and it was my lot to be amongst a disagreeable lot. We had time to get out and have a wash at some of the stations and we had refreshments provided at some of our stopping places and some of us had to break our temperance pledge as they had put rum in the tea. I believe I missed two servings but it was very little we got. And we soon began to see signs of winter and the sight of snow outside. The cold carriages had no lights or very few and where they were fortunate to have one, someone would kindly get to the top of the carriage and exchange for one without oil in. And a drink of warm tea was a treasure to us. We passed through Amiens, Lyons and Rully and the outskirts of Paris at night. And we arrived at a small station called Pont Remy at 2.30p.m. on the 9th of March. We had a cold dinner and a drink of warm tea after which we marched five miles to our destination, which was not a very encouraging start for lodgings in France. We were taken into a farm yard and allotted our apartments in the old outbuildings which were not very weather proof. But we soon found that some unfortunate soldiers had been there before us. So our first night did not go down so well as the climate was a great change from Egypt. But being soldiers we had to stick it the best way we could and say nothing, but I was very fortunate. I found a penknife while preparing my bed, open ready for action. So my gain was some unfortunate chap's loss; but I will take special care of it for him.

The next day I started with my chum as contractors for H.M. government and on the day following we had three inches of snow to greet us so we had to make the farmhouse into a hospital for sickness as there were a lot of troops stationed near, Indians and troops of our division. We had to be mudlarks now as sand was a thing of the past. I got a little hospital work here and we got all things straightened up when we had to do a move again. And well may John Bull call us the touring

division; we did not know where we were. On the 25th
March we began packing wagons and left the day
following and marched eight miles to Limeux. Spent the
night there and started at 7.00a.m. for Flesselles
arriving there at 4.00p.m. twenty-two miles. Had another
night's lodgings and left at 9.30a.m. for Beauval
arriving at 1.30p.m. Left at 9.15 the following morning.
And here I saw G Smith and H Firth. We arrived at
Vauchelles at 1.30p.m. to settle down for a few days. We
had nothing of much interest, only we knew we were
getting nearer to the firing line. We could see the star
shell at night and see our aeroplanes being fired at. We
only stayed here a few days and they were the worst
accommodation we had had so far. On the 4th April we
left for a place called Bus and I was very fortunate on
this move as about three or four of us went by motor car.
It was only about five miles.

And now for once in our lives we were in the firing
line within the range of the German guns. On arriving
here we had a busy time for a few weeks making suitable
places for hospital accommodation. And I soon realized
I had got amongst my Birstall friends. I met my brother
the second day and a lot more Mount Top boys the
following days. And on the 6th of April we had the first
experience of a bombardment which started at 9.00p.m.
to 11.00p.m. I think very few of us will forget it as the
earth shook and the elements were ablaze for two hours.
We had to start on action real as we had to take over the
trenches and dressing stations and we had always some
of our men in the firing line. And on the first Sunday we
were able to attend a Wesleyan service by Mr Martin;
we had some good times spiritually, as he was very
respected and very homely. And most of my work was

erecting huts and all kind of fatigues. And on the following Sunday we had the privilege of hearing a private preach from Sheffield, the Rev Mr Potts. He gave some very useful and sound advice. Just been relieved from the trenches he realized what man needed in the hour of trial and difficulties. And we kept getting wounded men in the hospital and we used to change our sections when they had been in the trenches two weeks.

On the 18th of April was my first venture to the danger zone, as we had to go for two loads of bricks from buildings which had been demolished by German shells. But it was a wet day and there was not much doing so we were not molested. On the 21st we got the news that the Russian troops were arriving in France, which was Good Friday by the way. And now we were having a bit of pleasure by having fine weather, as it was very discouraging to see the boys coming and going to the trenches, mud from heels to the top of their heads. It was a very dirty and dilapidated village. But we were very fortunate. We were in our own tents and had not the old barns for billets. And we were always kept rather busy in hospital as there was always something doing. Our boys were often making bombing raids on the Germans but it was very seldom they caught the Germans napping as we used to have a lot of casualties after these raids. It was rather amusing to see the boys before one of these raids – it was very often the Sheffield and Barnsley lads – to see them with their faces and hands blacked; their eyes used to glitter and teeth shine and their determination was strong. I well remember on the 4th of June the E Yorks and Y & L making one of these raids which was a great success. And the result was that we had eighty-one patients in that morning

52

which was Good Sunday; it is really surprising what great things in the army are done on Sundays.

It was very soon after this that I got put on to a more regular job in the oil and paint stores. My duties were to see to all the lighting arrangements, cleaning lamps, etc., and anything else that came my way. But it was far better than being a navvy and not very hard work so we got along very well. There was great talk about an important movement which was going to be made. Eventually the time came but for some unknown reason it was delayed for about two days. We got orders to send about seventy more men to the trenches and we went up on the Friday night 30th June and stayed at our dressing station all night. The bombardment had already started so we had to prepare for a night's rest the best we could in the barns. But it was not for long, what with rats; they amused us for a time. Then the Germans began to make us uneasy as they began putting shells very near us and it began to make the doors and roof rattle. So we had to move our lodgings into an old cellar, to rest not to sleep, as we expected starting for Berlin the following morning. I might have said this village was nothing but ruins as it was shelled each day[15]. And as night was passing and morning drew near, the terrible noise grew louder and louder, and we were not sorry when it was time to arise and shine as they very often used to say. So we got breakfast and spent the rest of the short time watching

---

[15] It is possible that he spent the later part of the night of 30 June in the building where I was accommodated, close to Mailly Maillet. Trenches traversed the garden, the cellar there had been used as a prison, and the place had served as a CCS / Dressing Station.

the bombardment which had grown more terrific. To watch our shells bursting over the German lines was one mass of smoke and flame.

At 7.30a.m. on that memorable morning of the first of July the boys went over the lid, as it was termed, many of them never to return; but it was a gallant effort and I believe if it had not been for our eagerness to capture too much the results would have been much better. And now we were beginning to see the early results, for the patients were beginning to stream down the road to our dressing station. These were wounded men who were able to walk, and by what information we were able to get from them, our boys were well over the German lines.

Soon we got orders to go and do our bit, and I can assure [you] there was plenty of work awaiting us and everything was strange to me as it was my first visit to the front-line trenches. We had all arrangements made beforehand. For anything we knew, we were going forward, and we had different trenches to go in by and to come out of. But the first we went in was not very encouraging. For a start it was knee deep in water for a long way, but nothing has to stop you in these times. And then we began to see the horrors of war, as our duty was to carry the patients from Basin Wood to Observation Wood. There was plenty of work awaiting us and shot and shell was flying in all directions and it was duck and dodge all the time. What gave us more work was that most of the unfortunate regimental stretcher bearers had fallen doing their gallant duty; their work was one worthy of military crosses.

Those who were left worked nobly with our assistance and the most cruel and arduous work was for us to go to the first line of trenches, which was very difficult and dangerous work as they were blown level in places and you had to cross in view of the Germans. We had to look very slippy in these places, walking over dead bodies and trees and machine guns and all kinds of obstructions and bombs by the dozens. But we worked on for four or five days with very little rest. The sights and sufferings of the poor fellows are not to be described. But they were very patient and wanted to get away as quickly as possible from the danger zone.

And often we were called upon to fetch men from dangerous places. I well remember me and five of my chums going with our officer for three koylies who were in a shell hole where they had been for three days. Just before dark or before they had begun to use their star shells they had been observed by accident by an officer who was sniping or looking for German snipers; at any rate he was the only officer I saw with a rifle in the trenches. He happened to see something move, and so later on he went to have a look and they had been lifting their water bottle up to drink which he had seen, which was no doubt fortunate for them as they might not have been found until too late. But they were saved so we began to get them in. As soon as we got into No Man's Land we were seen, as they started with their lights and the rat tat of their machine guns. So they brought the first one out and then it was our turn to go for the next. And I shall never forget the experience, like hide and seek, as each time a light went up you had to dive for safety. There were plenty of shell holes to hide in so by making a sudden dive you could very often escape before the lights burst into their brilliance.

I well remember the first dive I made. I landed into one of these holes and there I found there was a comrade. He was in a kneeling position. He had either been praying or looking over the top. I began to speak to him and shake him but I found the poor unfortunate chap was dead. So we had to wait our time to proceed, when we could see where our officer was with his charge. We got them out safely and by a difficult task got them to the dressing place.

The experiences some of the boys told us of were worthy of the Victoria Cross: of wounded men staying with their more unfortunate comrades to cheer and give them drink, and some to help them when night came on as it was murder to move during the day time. I well remember one poor chap who had brought one for about fifty yards, and with the wounds this poor chap had it looked impossible for him to look after himself. But I am afraid many of them will miss the distinction, with so many of the officers being killed, as they suffered very heavily.

About Tuesday things seemed to slacken down a bit and we got some good news that we were going to be relieved by another division. Things were getting busy on the right of us. By Albert there had been a bombardment going on for three days. And the words came true as our own soldiers had been driven back to their old position, not being able to hold the advanced position owing to the great losses. No doubt it was a start, and the Germans had very little peace from that date. As for guns and ammunition, we were well supplied. And we cannot give too much praise to our *men in the air for their noble aid, as their work was one of great daring. Our position in this Great War would have been perilous but for their observation and scouting work and giving the German positions to our gunners. Not counting for the waste of ammunition by the Germans who were constantly firing at them. They used to pay us an occasional visit by theirs but they were very rare compared to ours. We also had the observation balloons doing a good work, which was a great sausage-shaped airship controlled by a motor car and by different kinds of signals. I well remember them shelling one of our positions very near to our headquarters without effect. But they made a very good attempt and a few days afterwards a sudden thunder shower and a heavy gust of wind came and broke rope and it blew towards the German lines and came to earth in our territory.*

So we got relieved by our new division and on our travels back from the trenches we were given a reception by the German shells as they had the road marked for about three miles; but thank God we came out of it very fortunately indeed as we had about eight of our ambulance wounded but not of a very serious character. When we got back to our headquarters we had to start and pack up ready for moving off the following morning. This was on Wed night 5th July. So we left early the next morning and had a twelve miles march to a place called Gézaincourt. We got some very good billets and we started to make improvements, expecting to stay a short time, but it was only for a few days. It seemed very peaceful to be away from the noise of shells and the big guns. But we only stayed there until Sunday night and left at 1.30a.m. for another twelve miles march or more.

I might have mentioned visiting the cemetery where a lot of our brave men are laid at rest. These sights would be heartbreaking in peace time, but in days like these all the tender hearts seem to get hardened to such sights, as we had about 2000 patients passed through our hands during the four days, which was good work considering all the difficulties.

*Getting on with our travels we passed through Doullens to Frévent station and entrained there and had a three hours ride. Then we arrived at Steenbecque station and had another twelve miles or so to walk under a blazing sun. And we arrived at our destination Callone-sur-la-Lys. **And here we were like giants refreshed with new wine as it was like heaven to get back once more to civilisation**[16].*

Here we found very good accommodation both for hospital and billets, baths, etc. And it was only two miles from a town called Merville which we could get to occasionally by obtaining a pass. We soon settled down but we were rather alarmed as we got orders to stand to about the second day we arrived. But it ended in nothing, only us packing our traps.

I was very much struck here by the French people, more like ourselves, very strict at church services each morning at 7.00a.m. and they paid great attention to the sabbath day. They are a very industrious people. I often wondered why so many of the older people stooped so much as most of them seemed to be deformed in the back. But my curiosity was soon alleviated when I saw the way they used to work on the land; the cultivation

---

[16] My highlighting.

was a credit to them for there was very little waste or barren land. And it was the usefulness of a different kind of grain, maize or Indian corn and Arrocott [sic] beans that were their principal crops, and potatoes in large quantities. Most of the people seemed to be the owners of a few acres of land. You could see the women folk in a morning between five and six o'clock going to work and coming back at about eight at night. There was a lot of stooping in the cultivation of these Arrocott [sic] beans, picking out weeds, etc.

There were quite as curious sights as in Egypt as their carts or wagons were three-wheeled vehicles, most of them, with the one wheel in front in the centre, and sometimes with a pole but very often not. And their horses were very often cows and sometimes one of each, and dogs seemed to do a lot of lighter work. And your curiosity could be aroused sometimes by seeing them kill a pig. They would stick as we do and before many more minutes you would see them cover it up with straw and set fire to the straw and turn it over and do the same on the other side. And when they uncovered it, it would be turned into a black pig. And then they would throw water over it and begin a scraping operation.

There were many curious methods too during the harvest operations. And thank God for his care in giving them a good harvest and fine weather for the operations, as their threshing machines were like those we used to use some twenty-five or thirty years ago, steam engines drawn by horses. And you could see some of the people using the old method of the flail, the two sticks tied together. I have seen them in England but not in use.

As the weeks went by we got more settled down for staying a bit, and we did not care how long as we were

59

the only troops in the village. And they were very sorry to lose us. We had for our hospital a day school which was very suitable. And we began to indulge in sports of different kinds, cricket, football and fishing, but the latter was very dry work as about all we could catch was a cold or some the size of sardines. At other times you could fish all day and catch nothing. There were plenty of fish but they were more like the Germans, not to be caught napping. We also got some very good concerts up during our stay. We got a troupe of persons called the Popp-offs which was a very good take as their time was fully occupied going to different places to entertain different regiments.

There was great activity amongst our airmen here as we sometimes saw great numbers of them going to make raids. I remember one Sunday morning twenty-nine of them coming over. And very often they were to be seen in their teens. They were as common as birds to us. And it was our misfortune to see two of them come to earth, which had something wrong with their machines. One of the crew escaped injury but the machine was disabled and had to be carried away. But the other was more unfortunate. It came out of the clouds like a corkscrew all the way down. One of the crew was killed and the other did not live very long as he had his back broken and he died in hospital. We got orders to stand to a few times. But finally the orders came that we were to move the whole ambulance nearer the firing line.

On the 16th of September some of our boys left and the day following, Sunday again, we all had to move to a place called Locon a few miles distance to take the place of another ambulance. Here we were scattered about very much, although we were very fortunate for billets and hospital accommodation. During our march we passed over La Bassée canal and we stayed at Locon from the 16th Sept to Oct the 4th. Then we removed for about two miles to Essars but we did not stay at this place, only for one day, then to a place called Robecq and our stay was not for long here, although it was rather an interesting little village. Our stay here only lasted four days. And on Sunday, as usual, we were on the tramp once more, not really knowing our destination. On Sunday night we had about five miles' walk to Berguette station, and then we entrained, and finally arrived at the familiar place Doullens. We were getting very near to the place which we had been to before. We had an idea that we were coming back to where things were getting rather busy, by the motor lorries and ammunition wagons passing on the road.

We finally arrived at a never to be forgotten place called Sarton, a few miles from Doullens. The billets were anything but respectable and mostly open air treatment; you could walk in and out anywhere, either through the doors, windows or walls, and the roofs were no better. And I well remember an R.F.A. man coming through our billet and giving one of the walls a gentle push and it went over. It took about eight men to put it back into place once more. It caused rather a commotion as it was bed time and I had a rather trying time. I got a good billet the first night and the second I had to find fresh lodgings. So I made myself a hammock of two old hay nets and fastened it to the roof. It was rather a risky undertaking as I had some of my mates sleeping underneath me and they were more afraid than I was. But I only had one or two misfortunes with it when it failed me and let me down. It was a crippling experience

61

but it was better than the cold and damp ground. We soon found this was not our abiding place. We stayed a fortnight. During our stay I had the pleasure of meeting J W Farrard at Thievres.

On the 16th we moved from Sarton to a place called Couin, about another five miles. We were once more amongst the noise and roar of guns, a few miles behind the firing line. We had a very big undertaking and not at full strength, with about 400 patients with sickness, very few wounded. We had Germans as well as our own men taken with sickness; they were prisoners working in the quarries. They seemed like us fed up with the job, and we had no trouble with them.

On the 13th of Nov. there was a general attack by a few divisions after a few days' bombardment. Seventy-five of our men had to go to the trenches. It was my fortune to stay behind this time as I had a very busy task attending to the lighting of the camp, etc. for which we had about a hundred lamps of different shapes and sizes, and I filled my spare time up with other odd jobs when I had any time to spare which was very rare, only when there was a shortage of oil, so they would be after me the last thing on a night. I have known them come in a morning before I have got out of bed – for we had a decent kip, as we used to call it, spring mattresses and plenty of blankets.

As before our boys were blessed with good fortune as we only had a few slight wounds, about seven of them, and only one had to go away to the C.C.S; and one got the military medal. We seemed to be settling down for the winter months at this place as we began to make preparations for accommodation for 700 patients. It seemed to be the ambition of our C.O. to undertake *anything, whether we could keep up to it or not. The patients could not get the care and comfort which was needed, as sometimes two men had as many as sixty to eighty patients to look after day and night, which was far too many, whether they were serious cases or not. Most of our cases seemed to be the scabies, which was a very popular [sic] disease amongst soldiers. It was my conviction this was caused by lice and people scratching themselves and rubbing to irritation their skin until they made sores and getting dirt into them, turning them septic. We had all kinds of treatment, which was not a very pleasant process.*

So we laboured on at Couin until after Xmas, and to make matters worse they took fifty of our men to another ambulance to help them to make roads round their hospital and get stone out of the quarries. So we were about seventy men short and had between 500 and 600 patients regular, with about sixty or seventy discharges daily. Some of our hospital orderlies had too much work, seventy to an hundred for two or three of them day and night. I had no desire to go into the hospital wards as it was impossible to make the boys comfortable, what with cold and other discomforts. We could get neither coal nor paraffin, so the patients had to go neglected and the cooks were at variance. The officers were much more comfortable than the men, as much to drink and eat as possible and every other comfort most of the time. Had it not been for the patients doing what they could to help us we should not have been able to have done as much as we did.

Our stay was getting short at Couin and we were all glad to hear the news of our departure. But we had to spend our Xmas at the old place and it was rather a varied holiday, as we had all with the exception of one or two given two francs towards a good burst out. But like most of these do, it ended in failure as the boys were too early in getting their drinks. And it ended up as most of these entertainments do in squabbles and free fights, but no one was hurt. We had final orders to move on Wed. Jan 11th to a place called Beauval about twelve miles or more away. And I happened to be one of the fortunate ones to stay behind and ride on a motor car, which was very acceptable as it was no joke to march twelve or fifteen miles with a pack on.

We had visited Beauval on first arriving in France but only for one night. But we were more fortunate this time. It was for fifteen days and we had plenty of liberty to go round the town. I had a look through the church or cathedral or what they might call it. It was a credit to the architects and builders for the beautiful carvings and the stained windows and statues, and the marble arched roof quite out of the ordinary, with a beautiful organ and the player facing the congregation with his back to the organ. We got to the same billets as we had had the time before, but it was a crush up. But it only lasted two nights as we were all in one large room, about 220 of us. We were like herrings but we were happy and warm. But then we got orders to clear out and make it into a hospital. So we had to seek fresh lodgings, which was not too good as it was the fresh air treatment once again. But we used to cheer ourselves up with the thought it would not last for ever, and with the cheery news of John Bull and the Daily Mail of the coming of the end of the war. But to form my own opinion it seemed as far off as ever. We had our concert party going here *for a few nights. We had also some rough weather to contend with as it was snowing most of the time. It was rather a beautiful and clean place. But like most of the places which had been occupied for long by the troops, both buildings and people were degraded somewhat. It was amazing what our lads spent on foolish habits of French drinks, which was somewhat cheap but common. I am afraid it will mean the ruination of many of our brave boys. So we were out for a rest, and it was up to each one of us to make the best of it and say nothing, but look ahead to better and brighter times in the near future.*

After staying at Beauval ten days we were on the move once again and marched to a small village (Jan 22nd Mon) called Vacquerie nr Bernaville. We had a fairly easy time and during our stay here we had our divisional sports. But we had some very severe weather. Billets were good but very cold without a fire. On Jan 26th I put in a transfer to the R.E.Railways. After being at this place a month we got sudden orders to move on again. And on the 20th of Feb wending our way back to the firing line we stayed at Beauval, one night on this journey, and then had a long march back to the same old place Couin, the same hospital C.R.S. After about a week we had to send a lot of our men to the trenches as our infantry had advanced. They stayed a few days but there was very little doing. Soon we were beginning to hear rumours of moving again. And on March the 8th half of the ambulance went to take over another hospital about six miles away (at Maillet). We were staying behind until we were relieved by someone. On Mon 19th March we were relieved and moved to Orville for one night and then moved the next day to Beauval via Doullens and the next day to Blangremont and then on to Pressy nr Pernes, where we rested for a day. Then it was on to Fléchimelle nr Estrée Blanche, a coal mining district. I visited the pit head and on the 6th day we went on to Robecq. We [went] on Easter Sunday the 8th of April to a place called Allouagne and left there on Wed 11th April for a place called Bruay which was a big place and had been spoiled by the Canadian troops and refugees, a mining town full of sin and vice. We left there on the 14th for a place called Ourton. We were following the naval division and we were in reserve for Vimy Ridge to the Canadians, so we were continually on the move, not knowing our destination. [Marginal note: started a.m. stores] We left Ourton on the 25th of April for a place called Guestreville and stayed there until April the 30th.

Then we marched to a place called Anzin St Aubin about ten miles from Arras. We took over the trenches on the 10th of May, and about thirty of us stayed at H Quarters. We soon began to realize that we were in the roughest place we had visited in all our travels as every house was a mass of ruins for miles. From Mont St Eloi onwards we were just about out of the range of German guns, but we had exciting times by German aircraft visiting us at nights with bombs and machine guns. I paid a visit to Arras to see the destruction which had been wrought there on the 3rd of May and I soon found it was under German gunfire, as I had only been there a few minutes when I heard music in the air and I soon knew what that meant. My wonder was where their destination was going to be, when bits of shrapnel came close by us and bricks and stones were flying in the air.

66

So I cleared out as soon as I could. The night following an ammunition dump explosion occurred. Many casualties. I had the pleasure of seeing a German aeroplane brought to earth. The following morning we had one of our boys killed by a shell, the first we had lost, Pte C Hack [Golf prs]. Buried him on Sunday the 6th. His first time in the trenches.

Our division cut up. I met B Smith, H Firth wounded, [insertion, 'died']. We left Anzin on the 20th of May having had three killed and a few wounded, C Hack, Hy Vigan, G Whitman killed. H Mills left. Ruston W Watts, motor driver and one or two others wounded. We left Anzin for a place called Cambligneul nr Aubigny. We were to have a complete rest as far as hospital work was concerned. But you can always find work cleaning up these rest camps. It was a nice healthy country village and we could enjoy the country walks. Relieved by R N Div. Once more we began to think of leave as a few of our boys began to go, about one a day. We were having beautiful weather; sports, Canadian workshops. Left on Monday the 11th June. Back again to Anzin. Some up in the trenches, sixty. Not very much work. Fresh billets. We had some very hot weather. Aeroplanes very busy. Germans' machines – four – brought down the second day. June 7, Percy on leave.^{17} Left Anzin by motor lorry, June 21, for Ecoivres to work a C.R.S. Seventy patients and in two days about 300. The division and other two ambulances still back in the line.

End Of Diary

---

[17] Harry Atkinson's brother.

4

Echoes and Interweavings: The War Poets and a Voice in their Midst

How we read is clearly determined by what we have read before, a fact which is equally true of writing. This proved to be progressively the case as I read my grandfather's war diary. Following my husband's death in September 2010 and recognizing the need to embark on some mind-engaging project, I registered for a short, organised WW1 battlefield tour focused on the poets of the Somme, with the objective, quite apart from the literary interest the tour would represent, of giving me an insight into background and locations; for there had always been the vague plan in my mind to investigate the diary further. The tour was scheduled for September 2011 and was the occasion, in the interim, for my first true reading of the war poets, inevitably connected in my mind, at however far a remove, with my grandfather's diary. Though I had read the diary more than once in the years preceding and been moved by it, it was only in the light of recent events that it claimed a more central place in my thoughts and imagination.

The reading and re-reading of the poets, as of Harry Atkinson's diary, in the months following this first visit to the Somme, in search now of my own self-conducted itinerary planned for the following summer (July 2012), was accompanied at certain moments by odd flashes of 'convergence' which I can only describe as illuminative, especially so in the light of the growing poetic force which, as the war progressed, the ordinary tommy had assumed in the creative imagination of the poets referred to. Far-fetched the idea of convergence between the two types of writing may seem. Miles apart the language must surely be, and inevitably so, given the nature of my grandfather's upbringing, education and working life. I felt echoes, nonetheless, recurrent themes and reactions, and, on my part, encounters with words in Harry Atkinson's diary which assumed new resonances, enriched meanings in the light of my reading of the poets. Thus, some seemingly mundane details in Harry Atkinson's diary passed me by on a first reading, perhaps even in subsequent ones; indeed they were almost an irritating distraction from the real – shall we say noble, heroic? – business of war. Only gradually, my imagination broadened by mental pictures or images distilled from particular poems, did I realize how loaded with significance a simple word like 'lamp' could be and the sense of pride and responsibility the word could instil in one entrusted with the duty of lighting a newly constructed hospital or casualty clearing station.

Perhaps, in their turn, these perceived echoes and convergences shaped my own call to poetry which for so long had lain dormant and which required my own personal contact with the soil my grandfather and the poets had trod to be sparked into being. This sense of convergence, then, I look upon as a staging post in my own evolution to a new mode of literary expression.

This chapter, then, reproduces a selection of poems (or excerpts from them) taken from the poets referred to in the opening chapter who trod the same ground as my grandfather; undoubtedly others could have been included. These are set by the side of parallel moments rendered by my grandfather's pen which, by virtue of this interweaving and juxtaposition, will perhaps be read differently from the way they were read in the previous chapter. Perhaps, too, taken together, they will give a sense of closeness and fraternity that overrides divisions of class. As has been indicated, they serve too as a stepping stone to the final chapters of the book, which take us a hundred years down the line, to the centenary of this war to end wars.

***

Siegfried Sassoon's poem 'Trench Duty', with its evocation of the "splashing murk" and the sudden call for a stretcher bearer, echoes Harry Atkinson's first experience, on 1 July, 1916, of the front-line trenches "knee deep in water", of going over the top, and of stretcher bearing.

Trench Duty

Siegfried Sassoon[18]

Shaken from sleep, and numbed and scarce awake,
Out in the trench with three hours' watch to take,
I blunder through the splashing murk; and then
Hear the gruff muttering voices of the men
Crouching in cabins candle-chinked with light.
Hark! There's the big bombardment on our right
Rumbling and bumping; and the dark's a glare
Of flickering horror in the sectors where
We raid the Boche; men waiting, stiff and chilled,
Or crawling on their bellies through the wire.
'What? Stretcher-bearers wanted? Some-one killed?'
Five minutes ago I heard a sniper fire:
Why did he do it? ... Starlight overhead –
Blank stars. I'm wide-awake; and some chap's dead.

---

[18] *Poems of the Great War 1914-1918*, Penguin, 1998, p.32.

'At 7.30a.m. on that memorable morning of the first of July the boys went over the lid as it was termed and many of them never to return… Soon we got orders to go and do our bit… It was my first visit to the front-line trenches… The first we went into was not very encouraging as it was knee deep in water for a long way but nothing has to stop you in these times. And then we began to see the horrors of war as our duty was to carry soldiers from Basin Wood to Observation Wood… Shot and shell was flying in all directions and it was duck and dodge all the time. And what gave us more work was most of the unfortunate regimental stretcher bearers had fallen doing their gallant duty…

But we worked on for four or five days with very little rest. And the sights and sufferings of the poor fellows is not to be described.'

Spring Offensive

Wilfred Owen[19]
[extracts]

Halted against the shade of a last hill,
They fed, and, lying easy, were at ease
And, finding comfortable chests and knees
Carelessly slept. But many there stood still
To face the stark, blank sky beyond the ridge,
Knowing their feet had come to the end of the world...

Of them who running on that last high place
Leapt to swift unseen bullets, or went up
On the hot blast and fury of hell's upsurge,
Or plunged and fell away past this world's verge,
Some say God caught them even before they fell.

But what say such as from existence' brink
Ventured but drave too swift to sink.
The few who rushed in the body to enter hell,
And there out-fiending all its fiends and flames
With superhuman inhumanities,
Long-famous glories, immemorial shames –
And crawling slowly back, have by degrees
Regained cool peaceful air in wonder –
Why speak they not of comrades that went under?

---

[19] Ibid., pp.124-126.

Wilfred Owen's poem reiterates the horrors of going over the top (literal in this case) and of exposure to the 'fury' of enemy fire. The 'wonder' evoked in the penultimate line of those who have survived the engagement and 'regained cool peaceful air' recalls that of Harry Atkinson in the rest zone at Callone-sur-la-Lys, his epic imagery conveying the miraculous sense of release from 'hell' (in Owen's poem) to 'heaven', from the cacophony of guns to this haven of peace and silence:

'And here we were like giants refreshed with new wine as it was like heaven to get back once more to civilisation.'

Edmund Blunden in *Undertones of War* (a prose account of his war experience written some years after the event but reading very much as a succession of poems in prose) expresses a similar exhilaration and rapture as his battalion marches away from the Somme:

'You have now learned that light is sweet, that a day in peace is a jewel [which] kind nature will shield from the corrosion of yesterday… Greenness, even if it was only November greenness, was our dream scenery.'[20]

Returning to the 'corrosion of yesterday', in Blunden's case Thiepval, in Harry Atkinson's case no-man's-land close to Serre, there is a striking correspondence between Harry Atkinson's account of rescuing the three koylies and in the process coming across a kneeling soldier in a shell hole into which he himself had dived to escape a surge of shells, whom he has the shock of discovering to be dead, and Blunden's account of his experience in the trenches near Thiepval

---

[20] Edmund Blunden, op.cit., p.108.

of coming across a Scottish soldier dead but kneeling, facing East:

'Death could not kneel so, I thought, and approaching I ascertained with a sudden shrivelling of spirit that Death could and did.'[21]

A certain understatement in Harry Atkinson's account, for he has not time to let his emotions take hold and impede action as he awaits the officer's order to proceed, is to be compared with Edmund Blunden's 'reperception'[22] (he is writing after the event) which allows him to essentialize his emotion in alliterative language ('sudden shrivelling of spirit') captured or 'recollected in tranquillity', to use Wordsworth's phrase.

Siegfried Sassoon's poem *How to Die* completes this trilogy of solitary encounters with an individual soldier dying, or dead, and reflects the quiet dignity and unceremonious heroism of the ordinary tommy:

[21] Ibid., p.98.
[22] See Nicholas Murray, op.cit., p.249.

How to Die

Siegfried Sassoon[23]

Dark clouds are smouldering into red
While down the craters morning burns.
The dying soldier shifts his head
To watch the glory that returns;
He lifts his fingers towards the skies
Where holy brightness breaks in flame;
Radiance reflected in his eyes,
And on his lips a whispered name.

You'd think, to hear some people talk,
That lads go West with sobs and curses,
And sullen faces white as chalk,
Hankering for wreaths and tombs and hearses.
But they've been taught the way to do it
Like Christian soldiers; not with haste
And shuddering groans; but passing through it
With due regard for decent taste.

* * *

A very different poem by Sassoon, still on the theme of death, transports us to a hospital ward and the daily ordeal of those condemned to watch the wounded dying.

---

[23] Op.cit., Penguin, p.4.

Died of Wounds

Siegfried Sassoon[24]

His wet white face and miserable eyes
Brought nurses to him more than groans and sighs:
But hoarse and low and rapid rose and fell
His troubled voice: he did the business well.

The ward grew dark; but he was still complaining
And calling out for 'Dickie'. 'Curse the Wood!
It's time to go. O Christ, and what's the good?
We'll never take it, and it's always raining.'

I wondered where he's been; then heard him shout,
'They snipe like hell! O Dickie, don't go out'…
I fell asleep… Next morning he was dead;
And some Slight Wound lay smiling on the bed.

---

[24] Brian Gardner, *Up to the Line of Death, The War Poets 1914-1918, An Anthology,* Methuen, 2007, pp.124- 125.

The hospital was Harry Atkinson's more usual working environment. One is reminded by such poetic reconstructions of his hospital work at Couin, on his return to the front, and of his mental suffering in the presence of the sick and wounded who for want of adequate staffing were not able to get the 'care and comfort' they needed.

'We laboured on at Couin until after Xmas and to make matters worse they took fifty of our men to another ambulance to help them to make roads round their hospital and get stones out of the quarries. So we were about seventy men short and between 500 and 600 patients regular with about sixty or seventy discharges daily. And some of our hospital orderlies had too much work, seventy to an hundred for two or three of them day and night. I had no desire to go into the hospital wards as it was impossible to make the boys comfortable, what with cold and other discomforts. I could get neither coal or paraffin so the patients had to go neglected...'

In the light of his compassion and desire to bring comfort to the sick and wounded, his concentration on his lighting responsibilities and other practical tasks assumes all the more pathos. It is a further poem by Sassoon on the theme of death which, by its poetic force, transforms the simple activity of attending to lamps and lighting, so mundane in essence, into an act of human presence and sympathy.

The Death-Bed

Siegfried Sassoon[25]
[Extract]

Light many lamps and gather round his bed.
Lend him your eyes, warm blood, and will to live.
Speak to him; rouse him; you may save him yet.
He's young; he hated War; how should he die
When cruel old campaigners win safe through?

But death replied: 'I choose him.' So he went,
And there was silence in the summer night;
Silence and safety; and the veils of sleep.
Then, far away, the thudding of the guns.

---

[25] Op.cit., Penguin, pp.21-22.

As the following two extracts remind us, Harry Atkinson assumed responsibility for lighting early on in the Somme offensive and his skills were called upon as demands on the hospital grew with the ever-increasing numbers of sick and wounded. It may have been his competence in this field which explains why, on more than one occasion, he was held back from front-line work in the trenches.

'It was very soon after this [his first experience of a bombardment in April 1916] that I got put on to a more regular job... And my duties were to see to all the lighting arrangements, cleaning lamps, etc.'

'On 13th of November [at Couin] there was a general attack by a few divisions after a few days' bombardment. And seventy-five of our men had to go to the trenches. It was my fortune to stay behind this time as I had a very busy task attending to the lighting of the camp, etc. We had about a hundred lamps of different shapes and sizes.'

Harry Atkinson did not allow his mind overtly to dwell on death in his diary, whatever its omnipresence and the questionings he might have had as a man of faith. He is caught up in the business of living and performing the day to day activities required of him. There is, however, one reference to a visit to a cemetery during the march away from Bus following their four or five days' engagement around Serre after 1st July. This was somewhere near Gayencourt, not far from Colincourt where the poet John William Streets was later buried.

'I might have mentioned visiting the cemetery where a lot of our brave men are laid to rest. These sights would be heartbreaking in peace time but in days like these all the tender hearts seem to get hardened to such sights, as we had about 2000 patients passed through our hands during the four days.'

A Soldier's Funeral

John William Streets[26]

No splendid show of solemn funeral rite,
No stricken mourners following his bier,
No peal of organ reaching thro' his night,
Is rendered him whom now we bury here.

'Tis but a soldier stricken in the fight,
A youth who flung his passion into life,
Flung scorn at Death, fought true for Freedom's might,
Till Death did close his vision in the strife.

No splendid rite is here – yet lay him low,
Ye comrades of his youth he fought beside,
Close where the winds do sigh and wild flowers grow,
Where the sweet brook doth babble by his side,
No splendour, yet we lay him tenderly
To rest, his requiem the artillery.

* * *

---

[26] *Battlefield Notes, France and Flanders (Poetry on the Somme, September 2011),* compiled by Andrew Spooner, Skylark Battlefield Tours, p.46.

Reference has already been made to Harry Atkinson's attitude to the 'enemy'[27]. Except for that late instance when, in an uncharacteristic period of apathy as the war seemed to him to drag interminably on, he expressed pleasure in seeing 'a German aeroplane brought to earth', he looked upon the enemy rather as 'brothers' who had no more chosen their present circumstances than he had, who were just as much 'fed up with the job' as he was, and whose lot as sick and wounded prisoners of war he could sympathize with as much as with the suffering of his fellow soldiers. As an RAMC man, Harry Atkinson was spared the exigency to kill and thus the moral and psychological trauma that for many must have accompanied the act of killing and the sense of degeneration into creatures of instinct and violence.

The last two lines of Sassoon's poem 'Enemies' express the redemptive force of a look, exchanged here in death, but which might also operate in life, in combative action or a passing encounter beyond the battlefield. One remembers Harry Atkinson's first sighting of the enemy at Marseilles, their 'happy and contented' appearance perhaps a determining factor in his sense of the beauty of the scene.

Sassoon's poem combines the themes of death and reconciliation.

---

[27] See account of his arrival at Marseilles in Chapter 1.

Enemies

Siegfried Sassoon[28]

He stood alone in some queer sunless place
Where Armageddon ends. Perhaps he longed
For days he might have lived; but his young face
Gazed forth untroubled: and suddenly there thronged
Round him the hulking Germans that I shot
When for his death my brooding rage was hot.

He stared at them, half-wondering; and then
They told him how I'd killed them for his sake –
Those patient, stupid, sullen ghosts of men;
And still there seemed no answer he could make.
At last he turned and smiled. One took his hand
Because his face could make them understand.

---

[28] Op.cit., Penguin, p.57.

One sees in the poetry of Owen, Blunden, and especially Sassoon where the theme of death and self-sacrifice is so prominent, the social distance traversed through the war experience from their sense of superiority to and remoteness from the ordinary soldier to their solidarity with them – with [as Sassoon put it] 'the foot-sloggers loaded with packs, … the men that do the dirty work and keep us safe[29]. The concluding poem of this chapter reflects this closeness in the modelling of poetry through language evocative of the ordinary man.

---

[29] Nicholas Murray, op.cit., p.93.

The Redeemer

Siegfried Sassoon[30]
[Extracts]

Darkness: the rain sluiced down; the mire was deep;
It was past twelve on a mid-winter night,
When peaceful folk in beds lay snug asleep;
There, with much work to do before the light,
We lugged our clay-sucked boots as best we might
Along the trench…

… He stood before me there;
I say that he was Christ; stiff in the glare,
And leaning forward from His burdening task,
Both arms supporting it; His eyes on mine
Stared from the woeful head that seemed a mask
Of mortal pain in Hell's unholy shine.

No thorny crown, only a woollen cap
He wore – an English soldier, white and strong,
Who loved his time like any simple chap,
Good days of work and sport and homely song;
Now he has learned that nights are very long,
And dawn a watching of the windowed sky.
But to the end, unjudging, he'll endure
Horror and pain, not uncontent to die
That Lancaster on Lune may stand secure.

---

[30] Op.cit., Penguin, pp.83-84.

Harry Atkinson's diary, like the unsung testimonies of so many tommies of whom, like Harry Atkinson, some returned, others did not, sums up the simple-minded honour, decency, tenacity and quiet devotion to duty of the ordinary soldier who, mostly uncomplaining and sustained by humour, saw the job through and upheld the values of freedom and humanity.

5
1916 – 2016: Itineraries – Images Past and Present; Recollections

I Bus-en-Artois

1. Entry to Bus

2. First impressions

3. Picardy farm of M.Ponthieu, Bus

4. Barns, stables etc...

5. ...once used as billets.

6. Château, Bus, army headquarters in 1916

7. Sports ground, site of hospital in 1916
The remaining land in Bus was covered with tents,
for approximately 25,000 soldiers.

8. The estaminet *once used by soldiers*

9. Barn adapted as soldiers' cinema

10. Cinema screen marks

11. Cinema entrance and guichet

12. Bus church today

13. Graffiti: 'The Great War, 1916'

14. Track along which soldiers marched from Bus to front line.

15. View towards Serre

16. Luke Copse with Observation Wood behind which Harry Atkinson carried wounded to Ambulance Clearing Station

17. Cemetery at Serre

18-19. Was this the stretch of grass opposite one of the cemeteries at Serre where Wilfred Owen lay down one day and wrote a letter to his mother?

20-21. *War memorial at Bus with a notice on the continuing relations between Bus and Yorkshire, in particular Hull. My providential guide at Bus, M. Ponthieu (pictured here with his wife) maintains a close friendship with the third generation of a family in Hull, one of whom was to visit them around the time of my own visit.*

II Calonne-sur-la-Lys

'It was like heaven to get back once more to civilisation. We were like giants refreshed with new wine.'

1. Welcome to Calonne-sur-la-Lys

2. Space and silence: reality or art?

3. Fishing interludes

4. Maize and haricots: rebirth

III Beauval

'It was rather a beautiful place… We had plenty of liberty to go round the town.'

1. Victory memorial

2. Keys to the kingdom

3. 'A church...

4. ...or a cathedral?'

*'The beautiful carvings and the stained windows
and statues and marble arched roof'*

5. Adam and Eve in the garden

6. The Birth

7. The Cross

104

JESUS ATTACHÉ A LA CROIX.

8-9. Stations of the Cross

JESUS RENCONTRE SA SAINTE MÈRE.

10-13. Carvings of the Evangelists

14. Mausoleum and war cemetery

15. Harry Pass-Yorkshire Regiment

IV Couin

*1-2. An amazing discovery: the chateau of Couin,
where Harry Atkinson would have been working
during this most miserable period of his life on the
Somme*

3-4. '*The officers were much more comfortable than the men; as much to eat and drink as possible and every other comfort…*'

5-6. Places for the sick and wounded

7. The dining room, once the operating theatre

V Endings and new beginnings

1. Grave of J W Streets, killed on the first day of the Somme, the soldier – poet I would most have liked my grandfather to meet

2. 'Fin'? ('End') – an expression of hope or despair?

3. Resurrection

Recollections

My journey to the Somme was undertaken at a period of deep personal loss. I could not have imagined, given the nature of the venture undertaken, that I would return from it with such a sense of exhilaration and renewal, and of having come into the presence of a man, my grandfather, whom I had never known in life; he died in 1938. That, in the context of an engagement which had suffered the worst losses in British military history, 60,000 men killed or wounded on the very first day. Harry Atkinson was there to see the horrors and the mutilation, the terrors and the weeping, the cries for a mother or for God's mercy, as he carried the bodies to dressing and clearing stations. Yet his spirit survived.

Witnessing in our present age the destructions at Palmyra and other cultural sites in the world, and the corrosion of human identities that followed, I am made more aware of the part that cultural and artistic encounters – these, of course, combined with personal encounters, often unexpected, with a brother or 'pals' from his home locality he might have thought lost – could have played in the persistent regeneration of his spirit. Just as, I tend to think, his patient recording of these things played no small part all these years later in my own regeneration, as I traversed the places he had traversed and looked upon sights and images he had looked upon and reacted to, liberating new expressive impulses within myself which held loss and uncertainty at bay. This was nowhere more so than in the magnificent church at Beauval, unexceptional though its exterior might be. There, the images which had so inspired and uplifted him slowly fused in my imagination to form a composite picture symbolic in its power.

The images, then, form a story in themselves which brings to the fore in the narrative the dimension of memoir. It is a memoir in which two minds are superposed, at key moments interflowing, interacting, to create a new consciousness, a new way of reacting to events in time, poetic in intent. And time, at moments, seems to take on a hint of destiny as life finds shape, meaning, through encounters with others.

A major stimulus in my journey was, as indicated, the unexpected human encounters. This was the case from the very first stage of my itinerary: Bus, the village where Harry Atkinson like so many others was billeted

114

in the lead-up to the Somme and immediately after. As I drove into the main street, so barren, unlovely from my angle of approach, an ugly barn-like structure rearing its mass from the roadside and impeding any view beyond, I imagined the desolation of the soldiers, after their long hours' cross-country march, tramping into their destination, not knowing where they were or what might await them, for information, at least for the tommies, was in short supply.

But human encounters rapidly transform desolation and emptiness. Inadvertently trespassing on private farmland as I chose to venture up a lane at the far end of the village, I suddenly found myself face to face with the farmer. Happily a congenial man, on learning of my business he directed me to the homes of two people in the village who, he assured me, would tell me all I wanted to know about Bus and the Somme.

So it was that I made the acquaintance of M. Ponthieu who, as my first introduction to the village, showed me round his attractive Picardy farmstead, pointing out in the process particular places where soldiers had been billeted. Following this, he took me to meet his neighbour, Ghislain Lobin who, though a much younger man, was considerably more knowledgeable about local history than he himself was, he informed me. Ghislain's life was, indeed, steeped in the Somme. From his daily wanderings over the years through the surrounding fields and woods, he had picked up a mass of relics from which he had created his own private museum. He gave me one or two items from it – a beer and a sauce bottle, buttons and a belt-strap from a soldier's uniform still encrusted with soil, a dessert spoon – though the relic I remained most proud of was a piece of shrapnel I had found for myself in a ploughed field near Thiepval. Ghislain worked for the British War Graves' Commission, maintaining the cemeteries, replanting – every three years, I think he said – the roses around the graves, which made such a moving and beautiful sight. Through both of them I discovered, bit by bit, the hidden memories of the village as they are recorded in the illustrations above.

My encounter with Beauval was necessarily different, for I knew what I was looking for, or thought that I did. There remained, though, the nagging doubt that it was situated not far from Doullens. In my earlier travels through France, Doullens was a place I passed through as quickly as possible, identified as it was in my mind with derelict factories and chimneys and mines, the very name Doullens evoking in French the blackest of griefs. Ironic, then, I found it that Beauval, where Harry Atkinson had experienced moments of such high inspiration, should be situated only a stone's throw away. But, as I soon found out, it was in the midst of a landscape completely different.

As I descended on a fresh, sunny July morning from the plateau high above the town and surveyed the general scene, I was struck by the town's almost alpine setting of soft green meadows and neat hamlets connected by white, winding roads. But it was the church, not a landscape, I had come principally to see. And the church, on my arrival in the town square, I found to be stubbornly locked. Nor was there any chance of opening it, I learned on visiting the *mairie*, for the person in charge was on holiday; and that appeared to be that. As I hovered in disbelief, the door to the reception office suddenly opened and the mayor himself strode in. It was all that was needed to change the day. The mayor, M. Lucas, accompanied me to the town centre, then up past the church to the cemetery and huge mausoleum, a sight in itself, regaling me as we walked with the history of the town, from its former prosperity based on the jute industry, used for the manufacture of sacks. The factory, redundant since the fifties, was to be demolished the following week, he told me, to make room for the installation of a gas pipeline from Dunkirk, which would revive the town's fortunes.

At last he opened up the church itself. Hardly had we entered than the clock struck twelve, a sacrosanct hour for working people, as every visitor to France knows. He promptly handed me the bunch of heavy, ancient keys and told me I could keep them for the rest of the day.

So I came to survey at my leisure all that had interested and inspired my grandfather on that far-distant day: the architecture and carvings in wood and in stone, the marble and stained glass and wall paintings, the wonder I might otherwise have felt at the church's innumerable riches for so small a town explained by what I had learned of the wealth the town had accumulated over time. When I eventually emerged into the sunshine, I seemed to meet with a smiling familiarity at every turn, almost as though I was one of their own: the chirpy 'Bonjour M'dame' of a bright-eyed little boy emerging from an alleyway, the cheeky laughter and essays at conversation of three schoolgirls precariously balanced on a bicycle, who more than once as they circled round the cemetery walks accosted me 'for a light'… 'S'il vous plaît, M'dame'.

It was a remarkable day by any account, all the more so compared with the expectations of my forthcoming visit to Couin. This was the place where Harry Atkinson had been so unhappy, so frustrated by the inadequate staffing and indifference of officers, and by his own sense of helplessness before the unending spectacle of rampant disease and suffering, incapacitated himself by his lowering morale as the war dragged interminably on.

I expected to come across a drab little place. I found myself in contrast in an attractive tree-lined village situated on top of a hill, which fell away to lush undulating pastures and woods beyond. With its scattered ancient cottages and houses and beautifully kept gardens, it gave no indication of ever having been touched by war. Over a hedge, as I wandered along the main road through the village, I was confronted by the spectacle of a château gleaming white in the sun, framed by trees. An unobtrusive notice told me it was open that afternoon. At first the only visitor, I learned to my astonishment from the lady-owner who served as guide, that this had been the centre of RAMC operations in the locality. It was here, then, in these grandiose surroundings, that Harry Atkinson had experienced that dejection and cynicism so uncharacteristic of him, and evident nowhere else in his diary. The first room she took me into was the dining room which had served as the operating theatre, its present-day stillness and elegance making it hard to imagine the torments and suffering to which it had once been a witness.

Was it the shock of incongruity that dulled my senses as I later wandered around the park and gardens and stables, the private church too which undoubtedly held much of interest. These things had drawn no comment from Harry Atkinson. Was he sensible to the aura of class? The only positive detail of his stay here which stuck in my mind was that here, for the first time, he had known the luxury of a sprung mattress to sleep on. Couin remained Couin, a place that left my heart cold, except for the small sunny cemetery I discovered later down a side-lane...

Couin could not have contrasted more sharply in my mind with Calonne-sur-la-Lys, the place I knew would be the high point of my itinerary... Calonne, which finds its place at the very centre of his diary, where he had discovered the true meaning of 'civilisation', the name itself of the village suggestive of beauty and peace. A lover of the French countryside and of French rural life still grounded in peasant ways, I could not wait to relive with my own heart-beat the essence of his experience there. The explosion of a thunderstorm which cracked and reverberated all around me high on a plateau when I was roughly half way there, merely heightened my suspense.

My mood of enthusiasm, however, I felt suddenly waning when, the last stage of my journey reached, a road-sign indicating that this ideal village truly existed, I found myself driving kilometre after kilometre through an increasingly suburbanised landscape, with barely differentiated *pavillons* and flower-gardens bordering the road. When I eventually arrived in the village, it was to find not a soul, not a peasant in sight. Then it suddenly dawned on me: it was Monday, a day in France on which life is suspended.

So, with an empty heart, I resigned myself to my fate and wandered alone along flat dusty roads, with bare flat pastures on either side. All at once there was the sense of something different. The never-ending fields had given way to a large cultivated plot and I was standing by the side of a crop of maize and – was it? – haricots. Could this be the spot where all those years ago, day after day, Harry Atkinson had watched the peasant women toiling from dawn until dusk?

Whatever the momentary excitement, my mood barely resonated with the richness of life and impressions Harry Atkinson had known. As I turned on my steps to return to the village for an early departure, I was still an outsider, cut off from the past and the essence of things.

Suddenly, afar off, there was the drone of an aeroplane. It grew ever louder the closer to the village I got, as if our paths were destined to meet. As I came to the telegraph poles lining the approach road to the village, the vibrations diminished as though the engine was about to stall. I looked up in panic, for the plane was directly above me now, hovering between the parallel wires. Suddenly I knew and I waited in the stillness…

Everything is dim in my memory after that.

6
The Somme Revisited, Dialogue with the Living: Poems by Margaret Parry

The Stretcher Bearer

Not for you, the guts, the gore, the grotesque grins
Of those who've lost their innards, limbs but most of all
Their minds which told them but a few months past
How glorious 'twas to fight for king and kind
And made them look with pride into a spouse's or a
lover's eyes
Announcing that tomorrow was the day
They'd with their pals to the enlisting go
Declare their wish to fight for all
That's good and noble in the human soul.
You saw it all, the guts, the gore, and yet
Your heart would not succumb to words grotesque
To say what man was not,
A slimy mass of spewing sinews, gurgling spit,
Soft spongious balls that might have once been eyes
The mirror of the soul, but milky now, opaque.
All you could do for him who's lying there
In his last agony was kneel beside him,
Look into his eyes if eyes they were and
Not just hollow orbits staring blank
And hold his gaze in yours
Until his straining head reposed in peace
Onto a makeshift pillow that was once his pack.
He has a pal there standing by his side
Who knows his heart is still alive
And ready to fight on.

Entanglements: Dialogue with the Living

That's as it was surely meant to be
His first encounter with the land of France
Lulled by the rhythmic tramping of the feet
Borne onwards to a goal as yet unseen
Becoming ever softer as earth melts away
Suspends the shadows of his waking day
Composes, recomposes in imagination's eye
As it may yet still be some hundred years from now
Seen by different eyes
Beholden to the furrow and the plough.

A gently rising slope of ripening corn
Thick husky ears green shading all to gold
Stalks firm, serene as summer's eve passes o'er,
Sentinels to liberty,
Fringed here below, perfect, incorruptible –
For who would step into their loveliness? –
By blood-red poppies fragile on the stem
With blue-eyed scabious peeping out
Together with a myriad specks of white
Too delicate to touch, though she would like,
To feel that they are real,
Heaven's star dust come down here to earth.

Not those star shells on a night-time other –
The tramping long since ceased
Which one fine night had set his soul at ease –
He watches falling all around
Down into the labyrinthine mine where he is ground
Revealing wires tangled, bodies mangled,
Earth strangled, blasted heavenward…
Upward soars his vision to the rising sun
Where there is nothing but the leering, peering guns
'Quick, stretcher, over there, up over the parapet
And run'…

The Truth about War

'They had an easier time of it, the lads in the RAMC,
Not like the tommies in the field
Who risked life and limb at every sortie.'
That's what he turned and said to her that night
On hearing her discoursing with the lady on her right
About the man, her grandfather, of whom she was so
proud,
Fixing her with an eye, now dead –
A scar of war it can surely be said,
He was after all a fourth generation military man –
His word was law, that's what she read,
Let's get the record straight
Like the lecturer's just done on Menin Gate,
He who had scoured the monuments, knew them all by
name,
Those seventeen officers who'd never returned.
She wished she had never said a word.

He went over the top like the rest of them
On that memorable morning of the first of July
Lucky like his comrades to be young and alive,
Do his bit for king and country, not to mention children
and wife.
'A walk-over, it'll be,' the message ran down the line,
'not an enemy in sight,
Not even a rat, kick a football, if you like,
But hold your head high.'
Did ever one in the whole of history hear such a lie?

'They had an easier time of it, the lads in the RAMC,
Not like the tommies in the field
Who risked life and limb at every sortie.'
How could she deny the truth of what he said
When the man he referred to had come back alive
And the others were dead?

Desertion

Deep in the dank, dark cellar
Flat on a pallet, perspiring, waiting
For your day of absolution
Or is it execution?
Which means in my imagination
Hanging from a tree
But no, that's suicide
Yet better it would surely be
Than standing by a post for all to see
Until a shot blasts through your head
And that's the end of this brief life you've led
Because in an attack you got the jitters
And ran and ran
Yes, in your case you ran,
You did not leer, shudder,
So in your case it was judged
Not shell shock but desertion
That warranted not blighty, Craiglockhart
Or some place similar
With faces familiar
Who too had gone beserk
Not knowing in that moment who or where they were
This first day of July nineteen-sixteen
When you were just seventeen.

Above we are a merry gang
Sitting at picnic tables, laughing, joking,
Still not knowing
That down there it's a different story
Until now a thing most ordinary
That trap door we daily step over,
'Would you like to go down there?'
'Tomorrow, then, at nine-thirty.'

Down you were dragged over slippery steps
Deep into the labyrinthine vault
Bound, thrown on a board…
A vault, did I say?
One perfectly arched, modelled,
As the candle flickers high and flames
For us to look up in wonder
At man's skill, ingenuity.
For you superfluity.
Only blackness, a void, stones' tears, perspiration
Endlessly echoing, dripping
Fearless, persistent, like a crow pecking,
Its cavernous sounds piercing your skull
Till you writhe and you scream.
But who's there to know?
The door's slammed to long ago,
You're all alone and you're only seventeen.

Can't remember your name
Your initials – JC – are all I've retained,
But that is enough.
You died for the sins
Of all who do not know
That giving orders can be a mortal blow,
Destroy a man, deprive him of his senses;
For Christ's sake look into his face,
Pat him on the shoulder, show him that you care
And know that it's his mother he craves,
That he's not deserted, all alone in the world.

'A stretcher-bearers' post it was…'
Did you pass? Did you see?

Who'll pull the trigger to say it's a day,
That is, to signify the law's had its way?
When the question is put they all look away
These comrades high and low, who know what it's like
To get the jitters and run for your life.
But somewhere amongst them there surely will be
An aspiring young officer just waiting to see
What it's like to give orders, clear, unequivocal,
Not caring a jot men are born equal and free.

Calonne-sur-la-Lys

Say it quickly, essentially, say it
Softly, with a sigh,
Calonne-sur-la-Lys
Calossolis
Callos
Beauty in Greek

Not 'la lys dans la vallée'
Tempted as you might be
By the image of all that's lovely
In Indre and Loire's soft flowing streams,
Balzac fled from the conquering lure of Paris
To this landscape of ecstasy
Where woman appeared to him in all her mystery.

Here it is still the flatlands of the north
But wide marshy wastes now of reedbed and dyke
Far from the blasts and the cries and the groans,
A rest place, silence. But hark, there's a murmur,
Those women almost motionless there in the loam
Bent, prematurely aged but back every morn
To plant, tend, and to nurture
That life may go on.

Every morning he comes
To stand by the hedge
To look and to wonder
Not to utter a word
How can he, why would he
Break a silence so profound

Woman risen from the earth in her beatitude?

Calonne-sur-la-Lys...
What wondrous images carried her that morn
To where he had known himself a man newly born
Far from the Somme and the thundering machines
Man grappling with man, urged to hate and to kill
Or to raise on a stretcher and try not to see...
See what? Only now does he know:
'Civilisation' – the word is etched on his soul –
'Like giants refreshed by new wine we were.'

This rural idyll is what drew her on,
Women in sabots, rough frocks, foulards bleached by the
sun,
Eyes blue as the azure that frames and enfolds them
Glimpsed now through hedges thick with summer's
glory,
Honeysuckle, lilac, and flushes of wild roses.

Anything but this semi-urban sprawl
Meandering before her for mile after mile,
Not a lane but a road smooth and shiny as glass
On either side brick bungalows and villas, trimmed
hedges and grass,
Round bends, avoiding ditches, surely the next corner,
Hope rising, hope falling, not a sign to inform her...
All at once it is here, the village she craves
Steeped in the memory of him it had saved
The vigil by the hedge
Woman bending, toiling, rising...
Here there is not a woman in sight.

A flat gravelled square with a chip vendor's stall
All garishly painted in red, pink and mauve,
A solitary lorry driver perched in his cab
Gazing down as he eats, wondering what she's about
As disconsolate she traverses the desolate scene
Where everything's so different from what it should have been.

'La Clarence' she perceives on a blue and gold sign
Half hidden by geraniums on a parapet of wrought iron.
What a beauteous name! It's the name of the stream
Whose waters she looks down into
Flowing fast, flowing free,
Soft undulations of bright trailing moss,
Her first intimation that all is not lost,
Wander, yet wander,
For there is no saying
What's hidden there yonder
Where the meadow is calling.

It's long and it's straight, the dust encrusted road,
Bare and blank its monotony till afar she beholds
O'er shimmering haze of poplars silvery clouds unfold
Distracting for a moment from the scene here below…
But, oh! they are there, how has she not seen
These rows upon rows of 'aricots' thrusting up through the glebe
Whispering on through the years for one to believe?

How long does she linger? Who is there to say
Before she turns from the mystery, seeks another way
To return to the place she remembers all grey?
Lo, here's an old mansion buried deep in a copse,
In romantic abandonment, gate peeling with rust.
She comes to a standstill, as though caught in a snare,
A sudden inkling of something high in the air.

Now, unmistakable, it's the old road she joins,
Its two lines of telegraph wires strung high on their
poles,
With each step she makes the drone's more perceptible,
A small aeroplane is drifting down towards her,
Seems to stall, has another try,
Finds its level equidistant between the parallel wires
Perfectly poised now, hovering, as if holding fire,
Waiting for a sign…
All is suddenly so calm.

Calonne-sur-la-Lys, say it
Slowly, smoothly, softly
As a sigh
Callos
Calossolis
She looks up and smiles.

Stirrings of Poetry

The countryside traversed but yesterday –
Yet an eternity since then it seems –
Fold upon fold of ripening corn
Where Ruth and Boaz stood and dreamed
Like I once dreamed, a schoolgirl,
One of many in our form
But suddenly alone
As rapt I listened to her intone –
The French teacher, that is –
A poem,
The first essayed in this another tongue.
And suddenly I hung
To words and rhythms new
Soft cadences
Effacing all I thought I knew
Of this strange tongue
Till now a mere routine of learning, knowing.
I see her still on that far distant afternoon
A vague smile on her lips as she surveyed us all…
Leconte de Lisle…
The name is etched in me
As yet I see
A field of corn immobile as the noon
In shimmering tune
Inaudible
Thick lustrous ears in silence hung
To words as yet unsung,
Till all at once a breath, a sigh
The murmuring of an Aeolian harp
That ripples through

And they incline, these sentinels to beauty
As if to some lost deity.

In every village stolidly a church
Whose bells at hours immovable
Ring out the angelus;
Yes, still they ring from out the cavernous walls,
Keepers of rhythms immemorial
That made the landscape what it was
And would be still,
Or toll lamentably for one who's passed
And never more his gaze will cast
As homeward bound his tractor tops the hill
On tower or spire
Soaring o'er huddled roofs red in the evening glow.

There was a year when all that ceased to be;
One year? Nay more, but 'one year' says it all,
This arrestation inconceivable.
In that dread year they toppled one by one,
Razed by an instinct wild
Which stopped at nothing, would not even hide
Its will to mow you too in thousands
So much carrion to a land
Modelled – or so 'twas thought till then —
By God's all-staying hand.

A land scarred and pitted with shell holes, craters
Where bodies could be poured, obliterated
In one mass undertaking.
No individual tombstones to mark their passing,
Only torn excrescences
Which once were arborescences

Sole vertical element.

Until, against a jagged bole, the veil dispersing
I see you slumped in weariness, incomprehension,
Solitary,
The pals all scattered, gone
To different resting places, or those still left of them.
Your head is bowed in the apocalyptic silence
To sleep, or simply not to see?
But no, the swirls of smoke receding,
I see a hand that moves,
From left to right it moves and back again,
Now fast, now slow; now but a whisper, whimper
Like of a child who's cried its pain to sleep
And now reposes in a mother's arms.
Your head rests back against the blistered bark
Incarnate as the human mystery.

A dog barks in the night
To rouse me for a moment from my dream, then back
again;
Before I know a cock crow rends the morning air
And soon the whole community's astir,
Clogs, sabots, throbbing tractors all
String out the melody,
A patchwork of russet, green and gold
Glorious to behold
As too the trees and woods and coppices
That once upon a time, incomprehensibly,
They named Matthew, Mark, Luke and John.
Separate they stood but now they are all one
Like the field of corn aglow under the mid-day sun.

Epilogue: Convergence

It is moving to measure the distance, psychological and social, traversed by Wilfred Owen during the four years of the conflict, from his first thoughts on the outbreak of war quoted at the beginning of Chapter One, where he reflects so patronizingly and dismissively on all the 'poor Tommy Atkins' enlisted, whom he seems to look upon complacently as little more than gun fodder, seemingly lacking in 'brains' and 'temperament', to the image which emerges in his poem 'Miners'.

Harry Atkinson, like so many of Lord Kitchener's volunteers, was a miner. There is no more fitting memorial to their heroism and sacrifice during the long years of conflict, than the dream conjured up by Owen as he sits before the flickering flames of the 'hearth'… The hearth, the quintessential image of home, but charged now with all the unfolding conjoined images of mine and trenches rich with the alluvion of deep crushed bones and 'muscled bodies', with the shards of shattered trees decomposing to warm the hearth and hearts of after-years.

Who will remember them…?

Miners

Wilfred Owen[31]

There was a whispering in my hearth,
A sigh of the coal,
Grown wistful of a former earth
It might recall.

I listened for a tale of leaves
And smothered ferns,
Frond-forests, and the low sly lives
Before the fauns.

My fire might show steam-phantoms simmer
From Time's old cauldron,
Before the birds made nests in summer,
Or men had children.

But the coals were murmuring of their mine,
And moans down there
Of boys that slept wry sleep, and men
Writhing for air.

And I saw white bones in the cinder-shard,
Bones without number,
Many the muscled bodies charred,
And few remember.

---

[31] *Wilfred Owen: Poems selected by Jon Stallworthy*, Faber and Faber, 2004.

I thought of all that worked dark pits
Of war, and died
Digging the rock where Death reputes
Peace lies indeed.

Comforted years will sit soft-chaired,
In rooms of amber;
The years will stretch their hands, well-cheered
By our life's ember;

The centuries will burn rich loads
With which we groaned,
Whose warmth shall lull their dreaming lids,
While songs are crooned;
But they will not dream of us poor lads,
Left in the ground.

Sources & Select Bibliography

Somme battlefield tour 2011 and study notes:

(Andrew Spooner, *Battlefield Notes: France and Flanders*)

One week's personally conducted itinerary following Harry Atkinson's Diary, 2012; information obtained en route via personal interviews etc.

Family history research and related documentation (Kath Goodman and John Wriggles+)

Andrew Bannister, *One Valley's War*, (Outremer Pub. 1994)

Edmund Blunden, *Undertones of War*, (Penguin, 1928)

Henry Buckle, *A Tommy's Sketchbook: Writings and Drawings from the Trenches*, (The History Press, 2012)

Keith Gregson, *A Tommy in the Family*, (The History Press, 2014)

Matthew Hollis, *Now All Roads Lead to France: the Last Year of Edward Thomas*, (Faber & Faber, 2011)

Richard Holmes, *Tommy, the British Soldier on the Western Front*, (Harper, 2005)

Ralph N Hudson, *The Bradford Pals*, (Bradford Libraries, 2000)

Ernst Jünger, *Storm and Steel*, (Penguin, 2004)

Dale Le Vack, *Charles H.Horton RAMC, Stretcher Béarer* (Lion Books, 2013)

Joshua Levine, *Forgotten Voices of the Somme*, (Ebury Press, 2009)

Nicholas Murray, *The Red Sweet Wine of Youth: the Brave and Brief Lives of the War Poets,* (Little, Brown, 2010)

Martin Pegler, *British Tommy 1914-18*, (Osprey, 1996)

Sarah Reay, *The Half-Shilling Curate: A Personal Account of War and Faith, 1914-1918*, (Helion, 2016)

James Sadler, *Gardener to Fusilier*, (Helion, 2015)

Various anthologies of WWI poetry